SCHOOLYARD ECOLOGY

Teacher's Guide

Grades 3–6

Skills

Observing, Comparing, Describing, Measuring, Communicating, Organizing, Sorting, Classifying, Experimenting, Recording, Drawing Conclusions, Gathering and Interpreting Data

Concepts

Ecology, Ecosystem, Community, Food Webs, Life Cycle, Adaptation, Animal Structures and Behavior, Environmental Characteristics

Themes

Systems and Interactions, Patterns of Change, Diversity and Unity, Structure, Energy, Matter

Mathematics Strands

Pattern, Number, Measurement, Statistics, Logic and Language

Nature of Science and Mathematics

Cooperative Efforts, Real-life Applications, Interdisciplinary

Time

Five 45–60 minute activities

T 77665

by
Katharine Barrett
and
Carolyn Willard

LHS GEMS

Great Explorations in Math and Science
Lawrence Hall of Science
University of California at Berkeley

Cover Design	**Illustrations**	**Photographs**
Rose Craig	Rose Craig	Richard Hoyt
		Laurence Bradley

Lawrence Hall of Science, University of California, Berkeley, CA 94720-5200

Chairman: Glenn T. Seaborg
Director: Ian Carmichael

Initial support for the origination and publication of the GEMS series was provided by the A.W. Mellon Foundation and the Carnegie Corporation of New York. Under a grant from the National Science Foundation, GEMS Leader's Workshops have been held across the country. GEMS has also received support from: the McDonnell-Douglas Foundation and the McDonnell-Douglas Employee's Community Fund; the Hewlett Packard Company; the people at Chevron USA; Join Hands, the Health and Safety Educational Alliance; the Microscopy Society of America (MSA); the Shell Oil Company Foundation; and the Crail-Johnson Foundation. GEMS also gratefully acknowledges the contribution of word processing equipment from Apple Computer, Inc. This support does not imply responsibility for statements or views expressed in publications of the GEMS program. For further information on GEMS leadership opportunities, or to receive a catalog and the *GEMS Network News*, please contact GEMS at the address and phone number below. We also welcome letters to the *GEMS Network News*.

Printed on recycled paper with soy-based inks.

International Standard Book Number: 0-924886-35-8

COMMENTS WELCOME !

Great Explorations in Math and Science (GEMS) is an ongoing curriculum development project. GEMS guides are revised periodically, to incorporate teacher comments and new approaches. We welcome your criticisms, suggestions, helpful hints, and any anecdotes about your experience presenting GEMS activities. Your suggestions will be reviewed each time a GEMS guide is revised. Please send your comments to: GEMS Revisions, c/o Lawrence Hall of Science, University of California, Berkeley, CA 94720-5200. The phone number is (510) 642-7771. The fax number is (510) 643-0309.

Great Explorations in Math and Science (GEMS) Program

The Lawrence Hall of Science (LHS) is a public science center on the University of California at Berkeley campus. LHS offers a full program of activities for the public, including workshops and classes, exhibits, films, lectures, and special events. LHS is also a center for teacher education and curriculum research and development.

Over the years, LHS staff have developed a multitude of activities, assembly programs, classes, and interactive exhibits. These programs have proven to be successful at the Hall and should be useful to schools, other science centers, museums, and community groups. A number of these guided-discovery activities have been published under the Great Explorations in Math and Science (GEMS) title, after an extensive refinement and adaptation process that includes classroom testing of trial versions, modifications to ensure the use of easy-to-obtain materials, with carefully written and edited step-by-step instructions and background information to allow presentation by teachers without special background in mathematics or science.

Staff

Principal Investigator: Glenn T. Seaborg
Director: Jacqueline Barber
Associate Director: Kimi Hosoume
Associate Director/Principal Editor: Lincoln Bergman
Science Curriculum Specialist: Cary Sneider
Mathematics Curriculum Specialist: Jaine Kopp
GEMS Network Director: Carolyn Willard
GEMS Workshop Coordinator: Laura Tucker
Staff Development Specialists: Lynn Barakos, Katharine Barrett, Kevin Beals, Ellen Blinderman, Beatrice Boffen, Gigi Dornfest, John Erickson, Stan Fukunaga, Philip Gonsalves, Linda Lipner, Debra Sutter
Financial Assistant: Alice Olivier
Distribution Coordinator: Karen Milligan
Workshop Administrator: Terry Cort

Materials Manager: Vivian Tong
Distribution Representative: Felicia Roston
Shipping Assistants: Jim Orosco, Christine Tong
GEMS Marketing and Promotion Director: Gerri Ginsburg
Marketing Representative: Matthew Osborn
Senior Editor: Carl Babcock
Editor: Florence Stone
Principal Publications Coordinator: Kay Fairwell
Art Director: Lisa Haderlie Baker
Senior Artist: Lisa Klofkorn
Designers: Carol Bevilacqua, Rose Craig
Staff Assistants: Chrissy Cano, Larry Gates, Trina Huynh, Chastity Perez, Dorian Traube

Contributing Authors

Jacqueline Barber
Katharine Barrett
Kevin Beals
Lincoln Bergman
Beverly Braxton
Kevin Cuff
Linda De Lucchi
Gigi Dornfest

Jean Echols
John Erickson
Philip Gonsalves
Jan M. Goodman
Alan Gould
Catherine Halversen
Kimi Hosoume
Susan Jagoda

Jaine Kopp
Linda Lipner
Larry Malone
Cary I. Sneider
Craig Strang
Debra Sutter
Jennifer Meux White
Carolyn Willard

Reviewers

We would like to thank the following educators who reviewed, tested, or coordinated the reviewing of *this series* of GEMS materials in manuscript and draft form (including the GEMS guides *Treasure Boxes, Group Solutions, Too!,* and *Schoolyard Ecology*). Their critical comments and recommendations, based on classroom presentation of these activities nationwide, contributed significantly to these GEMS publications. Their participation in the review process does not necessarily imply endorsement of the GEMS program or responsibility for statements or views expressed. This role in an invaluable one; feedback is carefully recorded and integrated as appropriate into the publications. **THANK YOU!**

CALIFORNIA

Jefferson Elementary School, Berkeley
Andrew Galperi
Jan Goodman
Barbara Hopkins
Linda Mengel
Maggie Riddle
Fern Stroud
Beverly Thiele
Annie Tong

Malcolm X Intermediate School, Berkeley
Candyce Cannon
Carole Richardson
Louise Rosenkrantz
Mahalia Ryba

Fairmont Elementary School, El Cerrito
Nanci Buckingham
*Carrie Cook
Katy Miles
Nancy Rutter-Spriggs

Madera School, El Cerrito
Kristine J. Heydon
Janet P. Johnson
Laurel Miller
Anne Paulsen
Sue Ellen Raby
Nancy Smythe

M. H. Stanley Intermediate School, Lafayette
Mark Brune
*Glen Hoxie
Michael Merrick
Amy Wright

Multnomah Elementary School, Los Angeles
Sheryl Kampelman
Lucy Nigh
Elaine Peters
Connie Wright

Neil Hafley Elementary School, Manteca
Jill Durham
*Lesley Fontanilla
Dorothy J. Land
Nina M. Winters

Park Day School, Oakland
Harriet Cohen
Karen Corzan
Martina Kaumbulu
Michelle McAfee Krueger

St. Augustine School, Oakland
Diane Dias
Todd Jacobson
*Monica Middlebrook
Pat Schmitz

Stonehurst Elementary School, Oakland
Harriet Axlerod
Christy Grierson
Irene Herring
Claudio Vargas

Downer Elementary School, Richmond
Antonietta Franco
Lourdes Gonzales
Jennie Gragan

Grita Kamin
Eileen Malone
Galen Murphy
Emily Vogler
*Lina Jane Prairie
Marylee Stadler

Grant Elementary School, Richmond
*Terril Bertz
Kathy Clemons
Shelly Gupton
*Mary Mallet
Pam Roay

Wilson Elementary School, San Leandro
Jason Browning
Sarah Del Grande
Sue Reed Chevez
Maggie Swartz-Nierlich

CONNECTICUT

Allgrove School, East Granby
Tammy Chasse
Kathy Iwanicki
Kristi Smith
Patricia Smith

Plainfield Memorial School, Plainfield
Carol Bellavance
Laurie Brunsdon
Linda Gluck
Lynne Terry

FLORIDA
Gulfstream Elementary School, Miami
Adrienne Cohen
Fran Cohen
Robert Martin
Angela Taylor

IDAHO
Washington Elementary School, Pocatello
*Cathy Kratz
Tacia Tsakrios
Kathleen Wilike
Kristie Wolff

INDIANA
Lincoln School, Hammond
Linda McHie
Robin Miller
Tina Roznawski
*Barbara Walczak

LOUISIANA
Alice M. Harte Elementary, New Orleans
LynnBaker
*Janice Catledge
Marilyn "Cookie" Vallette
Margaret Wells

MISSOURI
Blades Elementary School, Mehlville
Sherlee Garland
Susan Jesse
Rick Livesay
Lisa Madigan
Dawn Meyer
*Susan Steinkiste

NEVADA
Dayton Elementary School, Dayton
Gail Bushey
Stacy John
Kathy Newman
Karla Rodriguez

Winnemucca Grammar School, Winnemucca
Cheryl Bishop
Maria Crawford
Naomi Menesini
Susan Putnam
Pilar Ramsdell

NEW MEXICO
Matheson Park School, Albuquerque
Gloria Archunde
Kris Donahue
Jayne Grant
Judith Gumble
Cynthia Themelis

NEW YORK
Public School 87, New York City
Miriam Ayeni
Leslie Corbin
Robert D'Andrea
*Betty Lerner

NORTH CAROLINA
Haw Creek Elementary School, Asheville
*Sandra Duckett
Donna Edmiston
Sue Jensen
Marta Johnson

NORTH DAKOTA
Dakota Elementary School, Minot AFB
Apryl M. Davenport
Linda Dickerson
Sherry Heilmann
Vicki Summerfield

SOUTH CAROLINA
Bryson Elementary, Simpsonville
Marsha Basanda
Melanie S. Helling
Lisa T. Hoffman
Linda Jennings

TEXAS
Harry C. Withers Elementary School, Dallas
Natala Assa
Sarah Jones
Liz Luester
Alex Rodriguez

Tom C. Gooch Elementary School, Dallas
Janie Broadnax
Flavia Burton
Harry Deihl
Kara Johnson
Tanda Pohl
Bill Wooley

*On-Site Trial Test Coordinator for *Schoolyard Ecology*

Acknowledgments

Many of the activities in this guide were inspired by the wonderful outdoor activities in the Outdoor Biology Instructional Strategies (OBIS) program, originally developed at the Lawrence Hall of Science (LHS) in the 1970s, and copyright, as is the GEMS program, by The Regents of the University of California. The OBIS series includes 97 activities in 27 modules. Portions of the following OBIS activities have been modified for the *Schoolyard Ecology* unit: Sensory Hi-Lo Hunt, Web It, Shake It!, and Ants. While the substantial intellectual debt to OBIS needs to be acknowledged along with our use of some illustrations and background information, the activities have been much modified by the authors, based on their own original contributions and the modifications made through the intensive GEMS local and national testing process. The drawings used in the Guide to Small Common Schoolyard Animals (page 73) are reprinted with permission from the Lawrence Hall of Science's Outdoor Biology Instructional Strategies (OBIS), copyright 1973 The Regents of the University of California.

We would like to acknowledge the original contribution of Kevin Beals, author of several GEMS guides, and thank him for permission to use his "Spider Web Key." We'd also like to thank Kevin for writing "Tales from the Web" especially for this guide. Other LHS and/or GEMS staff members who played a part in creating, critiquing, and testing this guide include Jacqueline Barber, Kimi Hosoume, Laura Tucker, Lincoln Bergman, Florence Stone, Terry Cort, and Vivian Tong. Ted Robertson and Kimi Hosoume provided inspiration, guidance, and many valuable additions to the activities and the background information.

Our thanks to Professor Robert S. Lane, of the Division of Insect Biology at the University of California at Berkeley, for guidance and information on the sections pertaining to ticks. Thanks, also, to Jan Washburn, Loy Volkman, and Steve Welter of the University of California at Berkeley's Department of Entomology and Parasitology for their scientific review of this guide.

Special thanks go to Janet Levenson and her class at Oxford School in Berkeley, California, for allowing us to photograph them participating in the activities, and to Libby Reid's fourth grade class at Mt. View School in Port Townsend, Washington, for helping us test the activities.

The excerpt from *Pilgrim At Tinker Creek* (page 57) is copyright 1974 by Annie Dillard and reprinted by permission of HarperCollins Publishers.

Contents

Introduction

Just outside your classroom window is a world your students can explore—filled with plants, animals, and interesting environmental features. Nature is at the doorstep of every school—even those whose schoolyards, at first glance, seem to be nothing but blacktop. Every school has ants, hardy weeds, and sunny and cool places that can be the starting point for outdoor studies. Direct observations of the relationships between the schoolyard environment and the organisms that live in it will spark students' curiosity about the patterns and interactions in nature, and will enable them, in later middle and high school years, to better comprehend and appreciate the complex interactions of greater world ecosystems.

Schoolyard Ecology brings together a combination of science and mathematics skills as students compile information and construct concepts about the environment. The key science concepts and skills developed in this unit align with national science standards and other current educational guidelines. During each class session, your clipboard-carrying student scientists work in teams outdoors to sample, record, and analyze information about organisms and conditions in the yard, and then return to the classroom to share and interpret their findings. Classroom activities include transferring data from student maps to a large map of the study area, journal writing, and discussions. Teachers have an invaluable opportunity to foster an attitude of discovery and stewardship of living things and to dispel common fears that some children may have about small organisms. Students are invited to reflect on the "value" of various organisms such as spiders and ants, as well as share ideas about why some animals are feared and disliked.

Throughout the unit, students use mathematics to measure, map, quantify, and classify their findings. The mathematical skills students use correspond to recommendations of the National Council of Teachers of Mathematics for this grade range, with particular emphasis on using maps, directions, and landmarks, and with going further suggestions for older students relating to scale, ratio, and grids.

Each of the five activities in this unit can be presented in one class period of from 45–60 minutes, except Activity 3, for which two class sessions are strongly recommended. Many teachers choose to extend some of the

An ecosystem includes all the plants and animals living in an area, plus the environment that supports them. A schoolyard is a small ecosystem.

Important note: For the best availability of spiders, ants, and other organisms, and for the comfort of yourself and your students, be sure to schedule this unit during periods of moderate weather. In many places, this means early fall or late spring.

For middle school students, this unit could be adapted to help construct a fuller understanding of the concept of an **ecosystem.** *Several of the OBIS modules listed in the "Resources" section would be extremely useful in this connection, and there are many other excellent units. The activities in* Schoolyard Ecology, *by focusing on interactions of specific organisms within a particular habitat, provide essential experiences for students. Over time, these experiences will enable students to construct a more* **systematic** *and complex understanding of the kinds of interactions that take place among organisms and the relation of organisms to the physical conditions of their environment.*

other activities to two periods if time allows. Several of the activities can be extended across the school year to become on-going investigations and individual student projects.

Activity by Activity Overview

Activity 1 begins with students exploring the schoolyard and mapping environmental characteristics such as dry and moist areas. Back in the classroom, all data is recorded on a large map of the study area. In later activities, as students add the locations of organisms to the map, they will reflect on correlations between environmental factors and the number of organisms in various places in the schoolyard.

In Activity 2, pairs of students locate, observe, and record the locations of schoolyard spiders and webs. During Activity 3, students sample the community of small animals living in the vegetation. Using a "shake box," they observe and compare the insects that fall into the box as the vegetation is shaken. In a concluding classification activity, students sort Animal ID Cards from this and the previous activity. Activity 4 focuses on ant trails and ant behavior. Students experiment with different foods and record the responses of ants. In a "Going Further" activity you may have students experiment with the use of different substances as possible ant deterrents.

By Activity 5, students are familiar with the diversity of life in many areas of the yard. Each student chooses a special area to study in detail. Using their skills of mapping, observing, and recording, students draw and describe their special study area. Writing and science are connected in this activity which can also provide an excellent way to assess student learning in the unit.

While a full and exciting unit, *Schoolyard Ecology* is not meant to be an exhaustive study of every aspect of the schoolyard study area. It is likely that many of your students will want to pursue their ecological class work—finding out more about ant society; investigating one kind of spider in more detail; learning more about the different types of nearby vegetation and the communities of small animals that live within them. There are many possibilities and directions. For teachers who want to expand the unit, or for students who want to pursue special projects, please see the "Resources" section on pages 81–92. We have also provided two short student field guides in the back of this teacher's guide that may be photocopied for use in optional extension activities after Activities 2 and 3. The Spider Web Identification Key, is designed to help students classify spiders by their web type (pages 76–80). A second field guide, Guide to Small Common Schoolyard Animals, helps students identify some common schoolyard insects and other small animals (see pages 73–75).

It is our hope that the famous biological phrase "the unity and diversity of life" will come alive for your students, as they see that even the smallest spot on their very own schoolyard is home to a marvelous multiplicity of life.

*Please note that these student field guides are optional, and are meant to be used **after** students have had a chance to observe, describe, and draw organisms for themselves on the schoolyard during Activities 2 and 3. Likewise, if your students will do additional library research about any of the organisms they encounter in this unit, it is best to have them do so after their own schoolyard investigations. Educational research shows that students learn best by first "doing," and then extending their understanding with related factual information.*

A Community

A community

Of interacting

Animals and plants

Want to find out more?

Here then is your chance…

It's not that far away

Just outside your door

Thriving on the schoolyard

Life goes on galore—

Insects, birds, and spiders

Bushes, shrubs, and seeds

Weave within the cycles

Of life's survival needs.

A community

Of interacting

Animals and plants

All are joined together

In ecology's great dance!

Time Frame

Schoolyard Ecology includes five activities in which your students need to spend time outdoors. The best time to conduct these activities is probably during early fall or late spring, during periods of moderate weather, when insects and other small animals are abundant. Try to build flexibility into your teaching schedule to allow for bad weather.

Activity 1: Exploring the Schoolyard Study Area............................45–60 minutes

Activity 2: Finding and Observing Spiders..45–60 minutes

Activity 3: Discovering Animal Communities............two 45–60 minute sessions

Activity 4: Tracking Ants....................................one or two 45–60 minute sessions

Activity 5: Special Study Sites...45–60 minutes

Activity 1: Exploring the Schoolyard Study Area

Overview

In this first activity, your students prepare to study organisms that live within the schoolyard by first becoming familiar with the place itself—with its variety of environmental characteristics. Students use their senses to observe environmental factors such as temperature, air movement, and sounds. Using clipboards with maps of the study area, pairs of students record areas of high and low moisture, sunlight, and cover. Through their observations and by pooling the class data on a large map, students begin to see their familiar schoolyard with a scientific perspective.

This activity also introduces students to field maps, one of the most important tools of the ecologist. By recording observations on their own individual maps and then transferring data to a large class map, students develop skills that will be used throughout the unit.

Ecologists have a wonderful challenge—there are so many unknowns and so many amazing pieces of Nature's puzzle to observe and figure out. This activity should stimulate students' expectations of the discoveries that are possible when they join forces to study the schoolyard ecosystem. Who knows what's out there?

Ecology is the study of how plants and animals interact in and with their environment. The word derives from the Greek "eco" (house) and "ology" (study of).

What You Need

For the class:

- ❑ 4 wide-tipped felt markers, in black, blue, and two other colors
- ❑ an overhead projector
- ❑ several blank overhead transparencies
- ❑ overhead transparency pens in several colors
- ❑ 1 large (about 3' x 4') piece of white butcher or chart paper

For each student:

- ❑ an 8 ½" x 11" piece of cardboard or manila folder
- ❑ 2 small binder clips or large paper clips
- ❑ pencil
- ❑ an 8 ½" x 11" student map of study site (made by the teacher; see "Getting Ready")*
- ❑ a journal or lined paper to become part of a journal

Note: Two sample maps are included on the next two pages. These are shown as just two possible examples—there are many other possible approaches. See Making Student Maps on page 11.

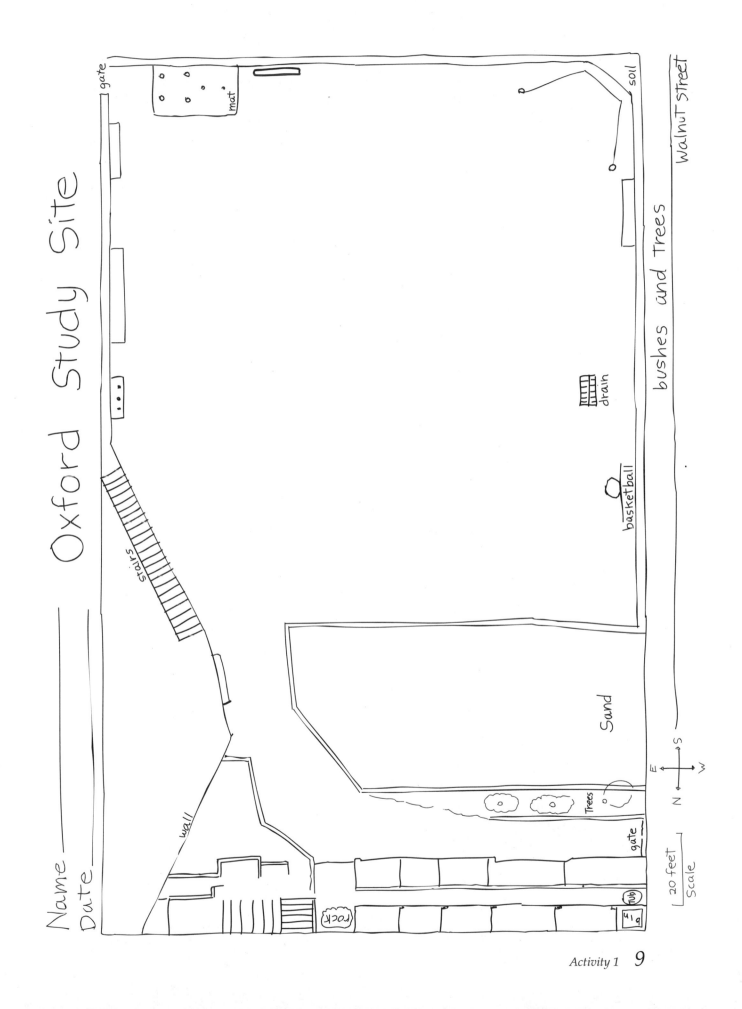

Oxford Study Site

Name

Date

gate

mat

stairs

wall

rock

tub

Sand

Trees

gate

basketball

drain

soil

bushes and trees

Walnut Street

N
E — W
S

20 feet
Scale

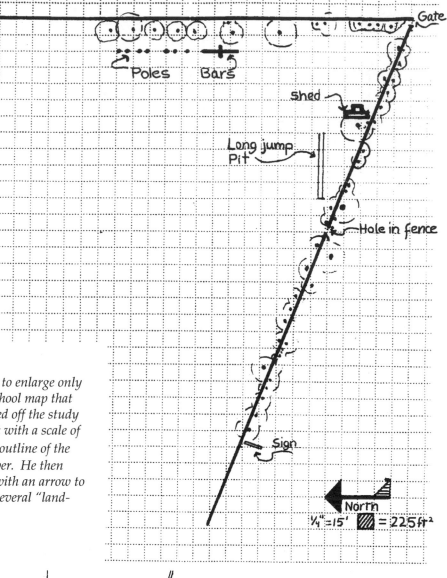

In one school, a teacher decided to enlarge only the upper, right corner of the school map that showed the study area. He paced off the study area, and decided to represent it with a scale of ¼ inch to 15 feet. He drew the outline of the study area freehand on grid paper. He then recorded the scale on the map, with an arrow to indicate "north," and drew in several "landmark" features.

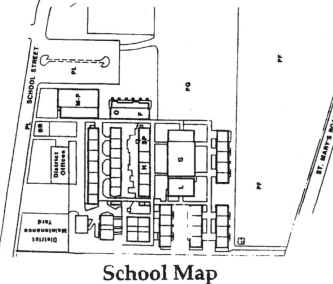

School Map

Getting Ready Before the Day of the Activity

Choosing Your Study Area

1. Choose an area or areas of the schoolyard with as much diversity of vegetation and as many physical features as possible. This might mean including areas off the play ground (near the school entrance, for instance), if students can be supervised safely there.

2. Take a tour of the area yourself, so you are aware of any potential hazards, such as wasp's nests, black widow spiders, poison ivy, poison oak, nettles, or ticks. (See the "Behind the Scenes" section on page 61 for more information about how to recognize and avoid these hazards.)

3. Try to build flexibility into your teaching schedule to allow for bad weather. Take recess, lunch, and P.E. schedules into account. If other students will be in the study area along with your student scientists, you might ask the other teachers to advise their students about what your class is doing.

4. Plan to hold class discussions inside whenever possible.

For most effective supervision, the entire study site should be within your visual range. Depending on your school site and your students' age and ability to stay on task, you may want to arrange for additional adult supervision so that students may study in several different areas.

Making Student Maps

1. Make a map of the study area on an overhead transparency. The map does not have to be extremely detailed or perfect; it just needs to be an adequate representation so students can record the locations of their findings.

2. If several teachers at your school will be presenting the *Schoolyard Ecology* unit, one teacher could make the map for all classes to use. Two possible strategies for map-making are:

• Get a small map from the school office. Enlarge the study area portion using the photocopy machine to copy onto the transparency.

• Walk through the area, counting your paces. Draw the area freehand on the transparency overlaid on graph paper, using an appropriate scale (for example, five paces to one centimeter).

3. If the schoolyard is very large, leave any buildings or spaces that won't be involved in the study off the map, so

Using maps to record locations of features relative to physical landmarks is the goal for elementary students. However, teachers of older students may want to include concepts of scale, ratio, array, and grids. Sixth grade students could draw their own maps on one inch or one centimeter graph paper. The large class map could also be drawn on large grid paper. Then, in later sessions, students could determine more formally where animals are most numerous in the schoolyard. They could compare the number of animals living around the edges of the schoolyard to the number of animals living in open areas. They could also find the area with the greatest/least number of animals per square foot or decimeter.

Some teachers use the projected transparency itself as a large map during classroom discussion and recording sessions. You may wish to use several layers of overhead transparency. The base layer would be the map of the study site. The environmental factors from Activity 1 could be recorded on one or more layers. Also, spiders, animals, and ants from the upcoming activities could each be recorded on separate layers of transparency. Then during class discussions each layer, or different combinations of layers, could be laid atop the map to allow you to focus on different factors or combinations of factors.

you can enlarge the area to be explored by students. (Please see the sample maps on pages 9 and 10.)

4. Include a directional compass and the approximate scale on the map. Draw and label some of the highly visible features, such as fences, bushes, benches, or drinking fountains, that will help your students orient themselves on the map.

5. Place the overhead transparency on the photocopier's glass to make a paper copy of the map for each student.

Making a Large Class Map

1. Make an enlarged version of the map by projecting the overhead transparency of the student map onto butcher paper, and tracing with a black marker. Alternatively, just draw the map freehand on the butcher paper.

2. You will later record class data with colored markers on the large map. So, if you will be presenting the unit to more than one class, you'll need to make a large paper map for each class, or have additional blank transparencies for each class.

Making Clipboards and Journals

1. Make a clipboard for each student. Inexpensive clipboards can be made using cut-up cardboard boxes, the cardboard backs of writing tablets, or manila folders and binder clips or paper clips to secure papers.

2. Purchase, or have students make, journals for recording their experiences throughout the activities. These can also be used for recording answers to the questions posed to the class throughout the guide. Students can refer to the written information during discussions. Teachers can use the journals for individual assessment.

Getting Ready On the Day of the Activity

1. Post the large map of the study area where it can be seen during the introduction and throughout the unit.

2. Have student maps and clipboards ready for distribution when you've finished your introduction.

3. Decide how you'll divide the class into pairs.

Introducing the Activity

1. Tell the class that they are going to be scientists searching for and studying animals and plants that live in the schoolyard. Explain that they will be finding a variety of small but interesting plants and animals that are common but often overlooked. The schoolyard will be the focus of their scientific work.

2. Introduce the large map, and say that it shows their scientific study area. Point to some of the main landmarks on the map and ask volunteers to identify them.

3. Ask students what kinds of living things (besides people) they have already seen in the study area and make a list of their prior sightings. [ladybugs, ants, birds, ivy, trees, grass]

You may want to keep the list of these organisms to compare later with the students actual findings.

4. Say that in the days to come, they will study the living things, but for today, they will go outside to learn more about the study area itself. Say that a place where things may live is called an *environment*.

5. Tell students that today they will get to pay close attention to what the study area environment is like. They'll *observe*, or carefully notice, certain things about the environment by using their senses of sight, smell, hearing, and touch.

For best results, keep this introductory session as short as possible. One teacher said, "I talked too much about concepts before letting the students explore. It's much better to save the discussion until after the students have done their observations."

6. Ask students to name some of the parts of the schoolyard that get the warmest, and some areas that are the coolest. Accept a few observations.

7. Ask what else besides warmth or coldness might be important to living things. List their responses on the chalkboard or overhead. Entitle the list "Environmental Factors," and say that scientists try to find out how these factors affect living things.

8. Be sure the list includes sunlight, moisture (or wetness), and cover. If no one mentions cover, add it to the list yourself, and tell students that cover includes trees, long grass, and bushes. Ask students, "What are some reasons animals might need cover?" [for shelter, hiding places, food]

9. Put "wet/dry" next to "moisture" on the list. For each factor listed, have students help you list the words for most and least. Here is a sample list:

Environmental Factors	Most/Least
sunlight	sunny/shady
moisture	wet/dry
cover	bushy areas/open space
air movement	windy/calm
Temperature	hot/cold
sounds	noisy/quiet
human activity	most people use/least people use
leaf litter	most dead leaves/least dead leaves

Explaining the Challenge

1. Tell the class that they will use their senses to observe all the environmental factors on the list, but they will especially study three of the factors—*sunlight, moisture,* and *cover.* Point out that animals also use their senses to find the place to live that best suits their needs.

Depending on the age and abilities of your students, you may want to have them map only one factor or more than three factors during this activity.

2. Explain that students will work in pairs (as two scientists), walking around in the study area. Each student will have a clipboard and map. The pair will focus on only **one** factor.

3. Divide students into pairs and assign one third of the pairs to each environmental factor. (It won't matter that several pairs are searching for the same factors.)

4. Say that if they're studying sunlight, they must find three of the sunniest places in the study area and three of the shadiest, and mark them on their maps by writing "sunny" or "shady." Review by asking how many places they'll mark on their map altogether. [six—three sunny, three shady]

5. Model how to record on maps. Ask students for a prediction of one place that might be the sunniest. If someone says, for example, "near second base," have her show where that would be on the large map. Say that she would write "sunny" there on her map. Take several more predictions, showing how to use landmarks to orient oneself on a map.

6. Check to be sure the "moisture" and "cover" teams know what to record. [the wettest and driest and the most covered and open] Say that if they have extra time after recording their factors, they should observe other environmental factors from the class list, too.

7. Distribute clipboards and a map to each student. Have them add the map to their clipboards, write their names on their maps, and walk to the study area.

Younger students sometimes have difficulty attaching the binder clips. You might want to have an adult volunteer clip on the maps in advance.

Exploring Sunlight, Moisture, Cover

1. Gather the whole class on the yard for a quick orientation. Ask everyone to locate where they are standing on their map.

2. Have everyone find north on the map, and then turn to face north on the schoolyard. Where are south, east, and west?

3. Point to a prominent feature on the schoolyard and ask them to locate it on their maps.

4. Ask a volunteer to review how they'll map environmental factors. [Record three of the sunniest places, three of the shadiest; do the same for wet/dry or for covered/open.]

5. Emphasize that they will be "on the job" as scientists, and that they should walk quietly and carefully observe several environmental factors. If your students are unaccustomed to working outdoors, remind them that this is not recess and that they are to use soft voices and refrain from running. Say that you will blow a whistle after about 10 to 15 minutes to signal them to come back to the classroom.

6. Circulate among the teams, giving assistance as needed. Help them locate big features on the map, then pinpoint smaller locations nearby.

7. Encourage teams who finish early to observe other factors from the class list. Signal the class to return to the classroom.

Back in the Classroom

The goal here is to share recorded data by transferring it to the large class map. If the sharing process becomes too lengthy, consider having the class begin writing in their journals while pairs record their data on the class map, one pair at a time.

1. Before asking for the data from their maps, take a few minutes for students to share any interesting discoveries they made about temperature, air movement, sounds, and other factors.

2. Congratulate them on their mapping efforts, and point out that scientists often begin studying an area by mapping environmental factors.

3. Say you want to record some of their discoveries about sunlight, moisture, and cover on the large map. Each pair of students will get to report *only two spots* they recorded on their maps. For example, if they're a sunlight pair, one partner will get to tell you where they found one sunny spot, and the other will report one shady spot. (Use the same procedure for moisture and cover.)

If you made your large class map on an overhead transparency, you can use different layers of transparency and different colored pens for each environmental factor.

4. Give pairs a few minutes to choose which two spots they will report. While they're deciding, make a key near one edge of your large map. In blue marker, write "Moisture." Write "Sunlight" and "Cover" each in a different color marker.

5. Gain the attention of the class. Point out the map key, and explain that you will use a blue "plus" sign to mark a wet spot, and a "minus" sign for dry. Ask pairs that studied moisture to share their data, and record quickly with blue pluses and minuses.

6. If students seem unsure about the placement of their data, prompt them with landmarks and directions. ("Was it near the basketball court?" "North?") To speed up the recording process, move your marker in slow sweeps over the map, and have the student call out when you near the appropriate spot.

7. Following your color key, use plus and minus signs to record the students' data on sun/shade and cover/open. When all teams have reported, ask, "What can we say about the environmental factor moisture (sunlight, cover) based on the class data?"

8. Ask, "How do you think time of day might affect some of the marks?" "What about the time of year?"

9. Ask, "If we go back out to the study area tomorrow, where do you think we'll find the most insects?" "The least?" "Why?" Accept all responses.

10. Tell them that *ecologists* are scientists who get to study the environment *and* the living things in it. In coming days, they will be acting as schoolyard ecologists.

11. If your students are the only ones using the clipboards, have them keep them and their maps for the next activity. If the clipboards are needed for another class, ask the students to remove their maps. Then collect the clipboards.

A Sample Map with Symbols

Journal Writing

1. Distribute journals. Students may want to decorate the cover of their "Schoolyard Ecology" journal.

2. Remind them to write the date and time of day at the top of their journal page.

3. Have students write in their journals about things in the study area that were interesting to them, and write down questions about things they wonder about or that rouse their curiosity or things they want to observe in future activities.

Going Further

1. Involve students in planning a weather monitoring program for the schoolyard. If you have access to outdoor thermometers, schedule teams to take turns collecting daily data to determine the range and fluctuations of temperatures. Students can make wind socks and wind and rain gauges out of inexpensive materials. They can check daily newspapers to compare their school site records with regional and local weather reports.

"One thing that surprised me was that our school's field area has such a variety of moods. One area could be quiet and shaded by a tree, with a warm breeze and the sound of birds chirping, while five yards away there is an area where the sun is blazing, weeds and prickle plants grow in abundance, and the sound of cars puttering echoes in your ear. Our field is definitely not just a large patch of grass."

*Megan K., sixth grade,
Stanley School,
Lafayette, California*

Activity 2: Finding and Observing Spiders

Overview

If we were to put all the spiders of the world on a giant scale, they would weigh more than all the people in the world! The vast majority of spiders are quite harmless to humans, and they play a major role in controlling populations of insects. There are thousands of kinds of spiders, many with amazing strategies for capturing their insect meals. The challenge of this activity is to find out how many different kinds of spiders inhabit your schoolyard and where they live.

Many children and adults are terrified of spiders, so it is important to establish a safe and positive tone for the investigations. It may be a relief to some of your students to know that the spiders in this activity will remain in their homes. This "hands off" approach is as much for the safety of these delicate animals as it is for the peace of mind of students.

Spiders are truly fascinating and productive creatures, and some of your students may become very curious and interested about the variety of their unusual behaviors. They also figure prominently in folk tales and creation myths, from Anansi the spider of African and Caribbean fame to many beautiful Native American stories—not to mention *Charlotte's Web!*

While continuing to improve their mapping skills, students use the scientific processes of observing, comparing, and describing. They collect and record data on maps and identification cards. The concluding discussion and the class map help students see relationships between schoolyard spider populations and environmental factors studied in the previous activity. An optional activity, in which they classify spiders by web type, offers students an opportunity to learn more about spiders.

After presenting Activity 2, one teacher said, "Next time I teach this activity, my attitude will be better about observing spiders. It was actually fun!"

Will your students find any spiders in your schoolyard? Teachers have told us that their students seem happy as long as they find even a few. Spiders are often common along chain link fences, nooks and windowsills of buildings, and juniper bushes. Try to schedule this activity before chilly weather sets in. Except for wintry schoolyards or ones that have been sprayed with insecticide recently, almost every schoolyard seems to contain quite a few spiders and webs. Wait a day or two after a rain, if possible.

What You Need

Some teachers have students use stick-on dots to record spider locations on the class map. Applying dots is quicker than drawing spiders, and dots can be moved if students make a mistake in position.

For the class:
- ❑ the large map of the site (made in Activity 1)
- ❑ a wide-tipped, colored felt marker—in a color different than previously used on class map
- ❑ 1 spray bottle filled with water
- ❑ (*optional*) approximately 100 ½"-diameter self-adhesive dots, all one color
- ❑ (*optional*) stories about spiders to defuse anxiety (see the "Resources" and "Literature Connections" sections on pages 81 and 99)

For each pair of students:
- ❑ (*optional*) 1 copy of the Spider Web Identification Key (master on pages 76–80)

For each student:
- ❑ clipboard (from Activity 1)
- ❑ pencil
- ❑ 1 student map of study site (made in Activity 1)
- ❑ 2–4 Animal ID Cards (master on page 30)
- ❑ a journal

Getting Ready

Since these cards will be used again in Activity 3, "Discovering Animal Communities," you may want to make another set of copies now.

1. Duplicate a page of Animal ID Cards (master on page 30) for each student, plus a few extra in case they're needed. Young students may only need two Animal ID Cards, so you could cut the page in half for each student, but don't cut the page into individual cards since larger sheets are easier to use on the clipboards.

2. Read about spiders, including ones that may be harmful to people, in the "Behind the Scenes" section on page 61.

3. Decide whether you'll do the optional Spider Web Identification activity featured on page 29. If so, you'll need to copy the Spider Web Identification Key (pages 76–80) for each pair of students and allow time for an extra trip to the study area.

4. Decide how to divide the class into pairs.

Introducing the Activity

GO !

1. Let students know that in this activity they'll again visit the schoolyard—this time to locate and observe spiders.

2. A good way to introduce spider studies is with stories about spiders, pictures of spiders, or with some fun spider facts. Here's an astounding tidbit from Alexandra Parsons' *Eye Witness Amazing Spiders:* "There are billions and billions of spiders in the world. If every spider ate just one insect a day for a year and you piled up all those insects in one spot, they would weigh as much as 50 million people!"

3. To avoid getting side-tracked by students' personal "horror stories" of spiders, invite volunteers to brainstorm some of the positive and helpful things about spiders. Also encourage students to suggest some ways that people can help others to become less fearful of spiders.

4. Ask students where they have seen spiders in the study area.

5. Point out that spiders are often secretive. Ask students to help you list some clues they can look for that may show spiders are nearby? [webs, egg cases, wrapped insect bodies, spider skins]

6. Explain that everyone will get Animal ID Cards to add to their clipboards. Depending on grade level and time available, say that each student should fill out at least two cards.

- On each ID card, they will draw and write about a kind of spider they find. Ask them to use descriptive words, and draw *what they really see.* (They shouldn't worry about it being artistic!) They should make a new ID card for each different kind of spider.

- On the card, they'll write their name, the date, and how many of that kind of spider they saw. It's okay if they don't know the name of the spider. They can note colors, too.

- If possible, students should draw the shapes of the different kinds of webs.

If you want students to do library research about spiders, it's best to wait until after the activity. Once they've made their own observations of spiders on the schoolyard, students will be better able to assimilate information from books.

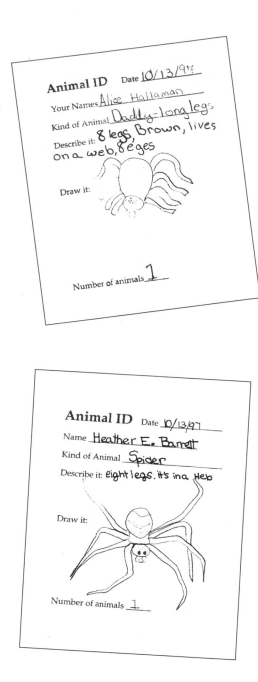

7. Be sure students know that they are not to touch spiders during the activity. Say that they'll be observing in pairs, but *each student* should do the following tasks:

    a. Search for and record evidence of spiders. Suggest that they use a spider symbol to mark the locations on their maps.

    b. Find out as much as they can about the schoolyard spiders without harming the animals or their webs.

    c. Gently use their pencil tip to touch a web. Observe the behavior of the spider.

    d. Fill out an Animal ID Card for each different kind of spider.

8. Divide students into pairs. Distribute the Animal ID Cards and, if they were collected after Activity 1, the clipboards. Have students add the ID cards to their clipboards, under their maps. Ask students to walk to the study area. Take a spray bottle of water with you to the study area.

Observing Spiders

1. Circulate among the students, encouraging their discoveries. Offer to use your spray bottle to gently mist webs for easier viewing.

2. Encourage students to look for webs, egg cases, and evidence of insect meals. Have them observe and report on spider behavior.

3. Remind students to draw and describe spiders and webs on their ID cards. Emphasize that they should draw what they really see, not what they remember from cartoons or books.

4. Remind them to mark the locations of spider activity on their maps.

5. After about 15–20 minutes, signal them to return to the classroom.

Recording Spider Locations on the Class Map

1. Back in the classroom, take a few minutes for a discussion of students' discoveries.

2. You may want to briefly introduce some of the information on spiders from the "Behind the Scenes" section. You could note, for example, that each different kind of spider makes a different web. Then ask, "How many kinds of web did you see?" Ask, "What's the same about all spiders?" [eight legs, two main body parts]

3. Draw a spider symbol in a new color marker (or apply a stick-on dot) on the key of your class map and write "Spider" next to it. Explain that each pair of students will get to draw a spider symbol on the map (or use a dot) to record one place they found a spider or evidence of spider activity. Say that pairs will take turns putting their spider symbols on the map while the rest of the class is writing.

If your class map is on a transparency and you are using multiple transparency overlays, have the students record on a "spider" transparency layer using a self-adhesive dot or a colored transparency pen.

4. Give the class 10–15 minutes to complete their Animal ID Cards and write in their journals about spiders. You might have them write a story from the point of view of a spider.

5. After all pairs have recorded spider locations on the class map, hold a brief discussion about what general conclusions they might draw by looking at the distribution of spiders on the class map.

6. Ask students to look at the data on the class map for moisture, sunlight, and cover. Ask, "Where are the greatest numbers of spiders?" "Why might that be?" [food sources, moisture, shelter] Ask, "What environmental factors seem to influence the spiders?"

7. Congratulate students for thinking like ecologists about how living things and the environment may be connected. Tell students that in the next activity they will be discovering some of the spiders' neighbors. Have students leave their spider ID cards on their clipboards, unless the clipboards are needed for another class. If so, collect the clipboards.

Going Further

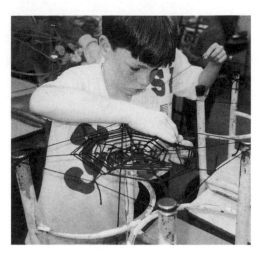

1. Try some spider math activities with your students.

    a. Gather class data to find out how many total spiders were observed. Estimate how many spiders might be in the study area. If each of those spiders eats one insect a day, how many insects will be eaten in one year? If half the spiders they estimate are in the study area are females, and each female lays 100 eggs, predict the number of baby spiders that will hatch.

    b. If an orb weaver spider uses 50 feet of silk to make its web each day, how many feet of silk will it spin in a week? a month? a year? Estimate a distance of 50 feet on the schoolyard, and then measure it.

    c. Reflect on the geometric shapes observed in webs. Design webs using yarn wrapped around the legs of chairs.

2. Drop small insects into spider webs and observe feeding behavior.

3. Locate and study spiders at home, both indoors and outdoors. Explain to family members why spiders are helpful.

4. Consider assigning "Tales from the Web" (which follows) as an optional reading for homework. You could invite students to write their own similar adventure story either based on what they actually observed, or what they imagine might happen. Remind them to keep their stories realistic. You may want to ask your students the questions found at the end of the story.

One teacher commented, "This is a good opportunity to teach respect for all living things. My students told their parents about the value of spiders in controlling insects, and encouraged them to refrain from using bug spray in homes and gardens."

Tales from the Web

The sun sparkled on tiny water drops on the silk threads. The threads were tight, each pulling and holding up the others. To a person walking by it was a beautiful spider web with dew drops, but to the spider it was a silk freeway, a tool for feeling things, a home, and a death trap for the insects it liked to eat.

The spider had a fat abdomen and eight skinny legs. Its jaws were ready to bite, and its fangs had poison in them. Its eight eyes stared into space. A fly flew near the web, but the spider couldn't see it. Its eyesight was poor, but its sense of touch was very good.

Its eight legs had stiff hairs that it used for feeling. Mainly, it sensed things through its web. It had special threads in its web that were very sensitive. If something touched the web, the spider could tell—just by the way these threads moved—whether it was an insect, another spider looking for a mate, or something big that might hurt it.

The spider stood there, without moving. The fly flew closer, but the spider still didn't even know it was nearby. Just then the fly hit a sticky thread. It almost broke away, but it made a wrong turn and crashed into the web. It buzzed its wings and moved its legs, trying to escape.

When the spider felt its web move, it jumped to action. It ran across the web on its eight legs, careful to avoid the threads it had put sticky stuff on. As it got close to the insect, the spider's spinnerets started squirting out silk, and its back legs began pulling the thick and sticky silk out, throwing it around the fly. The spider used its other legs to spin the fly around, while it kept using its back legs to wrap up the fly like a silk package.

The spider's jaws opened out to its sides, then closed as it bit into the fly's tough exoskeleton. The fly struggled, but it could hardly move. Its legs and wings were trapped and held down by the silk wrapping. The spider's fangs injected poison into the insect. The poison worked fast, and the insect died quickly. Even after it was dead, the poison kept digesting the fly's insides. The spider used its muscular stomach to suck out the fly's guts.

When it had finished, it moved back up to where the fly had hit the web, and began repairing the damage. Its spinnerets carefully squirted thin silk, following the pattern of the web. Later on that night, it would eat and re-spin the whole web as it did almost every night.

After repairing the web, the spider moved back to the web's center and stood still. As it stood there, a girl, who had been watching, accidentally brushed against the web with her backpack. Some of the threads didn't break, but others ripped and snapped. The spider curled up into a ball, and dropped out of the web by quickly lowering itself down to the ground, hanging from the silk it squirted out of its spinnerets as it dropped.

When it reached the ground, it ran across the leaves, trying to find something to climb back up where it could rebuild its web. It was almost helpless without its web.

A few yards away, another spider came walking up. This spider looked very different; its abdomen was covered with beautiful orange fur and its body was black. It would sometimes run to the left, right, or forward, and sometimes it would just walk. It was a jumping spider, and its eight eyes could see very well. It saw something moving ahead. It was the first spider.

The jumping spider might have attacked and eaten the first spider, but it wasn't hungry—it had something else on its mind. He was a male spider, and was looking for a mate. He walked and ran by. Sometimes he would jump, up to 40 times his own length. Like a rock climber uses a rope, hooking it to the rock now and then, the spider's spinneret left a dragline of silk behind everywhere he went. Every now and then he stopped to hook the dragline to something with little blobs of silk. If he fell, his silk dragline would catch him.

Finally he found another spiders' silk dragline. He could tell by the smell that it was from a female spider, so he followed the dragline, to find the other jumping spider. It took a while, but he found her. She was standing in a field, the sun shining down on her orange fur.

As he got near she turned around and got ready to fight. She was bigger than he was, and to her, he was either just something to eat or something that might attack her. He waved his brightly colored front legs in the air, wagged his abdomen, and jumped. She didn't move. He did it again. Something in her jumping spider brain told her not to attack. Instead, she waved her legs to signal him to come over.

The male spider saw her wave, and came closer. Earlier he had built a sperm web and dipped his pedipalps in it. He sat on the female's back, reached under her, and put his pedipalps in her pockets. They didn't know it, but they had just prepared the way for hundreds of baby jumping spiders to be born in a few weeks!

Just then the two spiders were scared by something big moving. It was the girl who had been sitting still nearby, watching everything happen. Feeling scared, both the jumping spiders lifted up their pedipalps, to make themselves look as big and scary as possible. To the girl they didn't look scary. To her they looked like two football referees dressed in orange, signaling a touchdown as they each held up their two pedipalps! She smiled, then stood and watched them a little while longer.

After a while, the spiders weren't scared anymore and they moved away, sometimes walking and sometimes running in different directions. The girl left them and went back to her science classroom. She sat down at her desk and pulled out a pen and paper and began writing… "The sun sparkled on tiny water drops on the silk threads. The threads were tight, each pulling and holding up the others…"

QUESTIONS:

1. How did the orb spider avoid getting stuck in its own web?
2. How did the orb spider sense the world around it?
3. How did the jumping spider sense the world around it?
4. What did the orb spider do to protect itself from falling?
5. How did the orb spider trap and eat the fly?
6. How did the jumping spider convince the female not to eat him?
7. What did the jumping spiders do when they were scared by the girl?
8. How was the jumping spider different from the orb spider?

Optional Spider Web Identification Activity

$\mathcal{K}$eying spiders by species is a difficult task. However, your students can use the information on pages 76–80 to classify schoolyard spiders by whether or not they have webs, and by the type of web they spin. These Spider Web Identification Key pages also include descriptions of several common types of spiders without webs. The pages also help students distinguish between two look-a-likes—Daddy-long-legs, which are spiders and Harvestmen, which aren't.

Give each pair of students a stapled copy of the Spider Web Identification Key (pages 76–80). Before going outside again, they may be able to classify some of their spider ID cards by comparing them with the information on web types. Then, have students take the Web Identification pages outside again to see if they can find and identify several different types of webs. Have them record the type of spiders they find in the appropriate places on their maps.

Note: This key will allow your students to identify some major groups of spiders, and learn some fun facts about them. Mating and courtship among spiders is an important part of their natural history and we include some of this information.

Animal ID Date _____

Name _____

Kind of Animal _____

Describe it:

Draw it:

Number of animals _____

Animal ID Date _____

Name _____

Kind of Animal _____

Describe it:

Draw it:

Number of animals _____

Animal ID Date _____

Name _____

Kind of Animal _____

Describe it:

Draw it:

Number of animals _____

Animal ID Date _____

Name _____

Kind of Animal _____

Describe it:

Draw it:

Number of animals _____

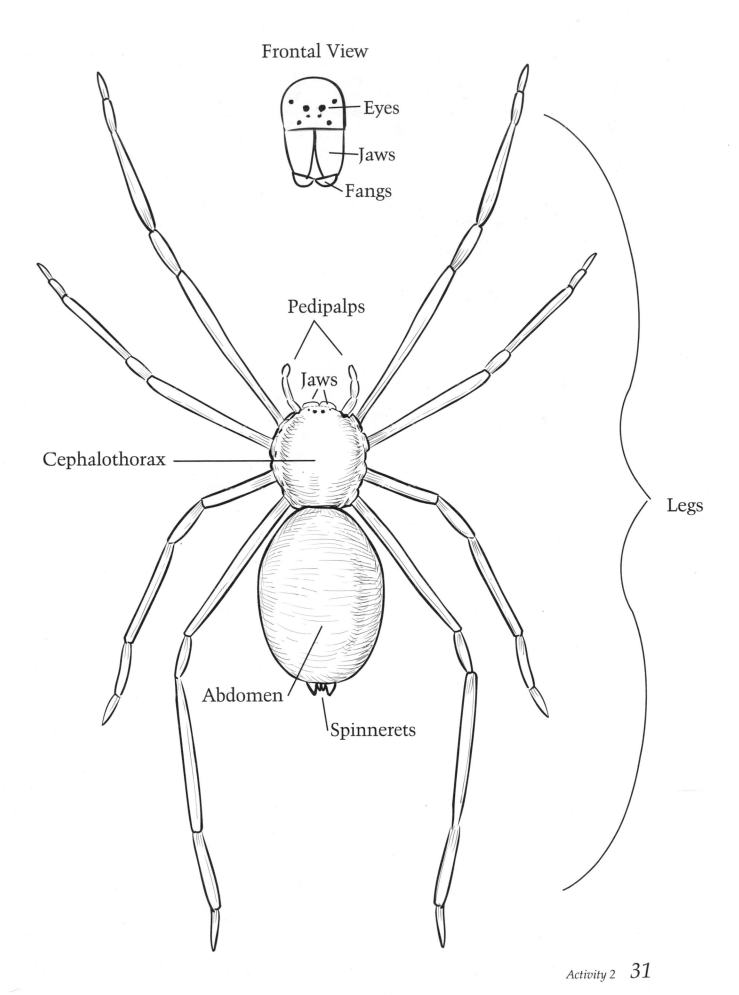

Frontal View

Eyes

Jaws

Fangs

Pedipalps

Jaws

Cephalothorax

Legs

Abdomen

Spinnerets

Activity 3: Discovering Animal Communities

Overview

This exciting activity may span two or even three class sessions. Pairs of students use a "shake box" to sample and study more closely a variety of small schoolyard animals such as insects. One student holds the box under a branch or tuft of grass while the other shakes the vegetation. As animals fall into the box, it is tipped and the animals slide down into the attached plastic bag. The bag is then folded back against the white background of the box, trapping the animals temporarily so they can be easily observed.

Students will be amazed by how many different creatures slide into the bag. A typical catch includes varieties of leaf hoppers, moths, midge flies, caterpillars, spiders, and beetles. The students observe and describe the small animals on Animal ID Cards. They record the location of each animal on their maps, and then release the animals back onto their home plant.

Back in the classroom, the class shares its findings, and students begin to explore the concepts of food chains and the interdependence of animal communities and plants in an ecosystem. After writing in journals and recording their data on the class map, students develop their own systems for sorting and classifying the Animal ID Cards.

One teacher said, "Frankly, I thought the animals on our yard were not that diverse or plentiful, but there was plenty to excite the students."

A population is a number of all the same kind of animals. A community is a group of different kinds of animals who live in the same area.

What You Need

For the class:
- ❏ the large map of the site (made in Activity 1)
- ❏ a wide-tipped, colored felt marker—in a color different than previously used on class map
- ❏ a large piece of chart paper or a blank overhead transparency
- ❏ a few magnifying lenses
- ❏ a dispenser of transparent adhesive tape (to repair shake boxes in the study area)
- ❏ (*optional*) field guides for common insects and invertebrates

For each pair of students:
- ❏ 1 shake box (see "Getting Ready")
- ❏ 1 pair of scissors for the sorting activity

For each student:
- ❏ clipboard (from Activity 1)
- ❏ pencil
- ❏ 1 student map of study site (made in Activity 1)
- ❏ a page of Animal ID Cards (master on page 30)
- ❏ a journal

Getting Ready

1. Make one shake box for each pair of students:

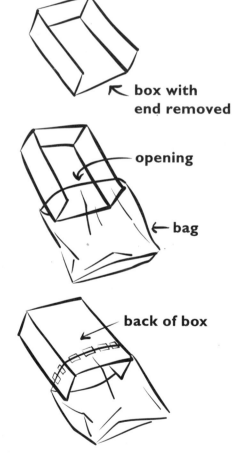

box with end removed

opening

← bag

back of box

a. Collect 8 or 9 small white shirt boxes (about 8" x 12"). The type department stores use to wrap gifts are ideal, because both the top and bottom may be used, thereby providing two shake boxes.

b. If the boxes are not white, you will need to cover both the inside and back side of the box with white paper.

c. Remove one end of each box.

d. Collect 16–18 clear plastic produce bags or purchase a box of plastic bags that come in a roll and are 8"–9" wide. Clear bags without any printing or logos on them are best.

e. Tape one edge of a plastic bag along the back side of the box at the open end.

2. Practice using a shake box outdoors before the activity. Using the procedure described in "Introducing the Activity in the Classroom," below, sample a few areas of the study area yourself.

3. Duplicate a page of Animal ID Cards (master on page 30) for each student, plus a few extra.

4. Decide how to divide the class into pairs.

Introducing the Activity in the Classroom

1. Ask students what kinds of animals they have seen in the schoolyard, either while they were observing spiders, or any other time. List these on large chart paper or an overhead transparency.

2. Say that today, they will again be acting as ecologists, looking for any small animals in the study area.

3. Focus the students on the class map, and ask where they think they'll find the most small animals. Ask them to think about environmental factors such as moisture, sunlight, or cover as they predict. Accept all predictions about where animals will be found. The students' predictions can be recorded in their journals.

4. Ask the class also to think about where in the study area they found most of the spiders. Ask, "What do you think spiders eat?" [They eat small animals like insects and other spiders—but not plants.] Suggest that students might find other small animals near spiders.

5. Divide the students into pairs. Let them know that if they want to, they can carefully turn over leaves, rocks, or logs to find animals, but they need to follow some guidelines (see margin note). To find animals in trees or bushes, they will use a shake box, which you will show them how to use outside.

6. Point to a place on the large map near a shrub, bush, or other vegetation where they will gather for your demonstration of how to use a shake box.

7. Distribute the Animal ID Cards and, if they were collected after Activity 2, the clipboards. Have students add the ID cards to their clipboards. Ask the students to gather their clipboards and pencils, then walk to the study site. Take along the stack of shake boxes, a few magnifying lenses, and the transparent tape to make any necessary repairs to the shake boxes.

Be sure the students realize that the term "animals" includes insects, birds, and amphibians, as well as mammals.

Some people are very frightened of insects. Point out that the insects they'll study are very small and will be inside a plastic bag. Encourage students who are comfortable around small creatures to help their classmates.

Make students aware of these safety and environmental guidelines— don't put your hands where you can't see (in case a dangerous organism, such as a black widow or scorpion is there); always lift a rock up from its other side toward you (in the unlikely event something might jump out, it would not jump toward you); and always return the rock or log gently to its place, so as not to harm the inhabitants. The damp, shaded habitat provided by a log is destroyed if it is not returned to its original place.

Modeling the Shake Box Outside

1. Gather the class around a shrub, bush, or other clump of vegetation in the study area.

2. Model how to use a shake box:

   a. Show students how to shake vegetation over the shake box (asking them to shake carefully so the plant is not damaged). Hold the box under the branch with one hand, and give a few vigorous shakes to the branch with the other hand. Explain that with the pairs of students, one partner will hold the box while the other shakes the vegetation.

   b. Show how to quickly tip the box so any small animals that fall on the box will slide into the bag.

   c. Hold the bag against the white back of the box to trap the animals. Also, it is easier to see the animals when viewed against the white background. Suggest that students keep the bag out of the direct sun so it doesn't get too hot inside.

   d. Say that after they have studied the animals and drawn and described them on an ID card, they will let the animals go in the same place where they found them.

   e. Show how to gently release the animals back into their community by opening the bag upside down over the bush.

3. Stress the importance of recording observations. When they find an animal, they should record on their map where it was found, and fill out an Animal ID Card about that animal. Also they should write on each card their name, the date, and how many of that animal they found.

4. Tell them that if they find tiny animals that are hard to see, you'll lend them a magnifying lens.

5. Let the students know that they'll have about 20–30 minutes to collect, observe, record, and release animals. Remind them to keep you in sight, and to be on the alert for your signal to go inside.

Sampling with Shake Boxes in the Study Area

1. Distribute shake boxes and have the pairs of students begin.

Back of Box

Most teachers recommend letting students use magnifying lenses outdoors only under supervision. Students are sometimes tempted to "fry" insects or burn paper by focusing sunlight with magnifiers.

2. Circulate among the pairs, noting their discoveries and encouraging them to share the tasks of collecting and recording. Offer lenses to students as needed, collecting them again as you move on.

3. Encourage pairs to show each other what they found. This can often be quite exciting and students are likely to observe differences in the kinds of animals found on different kinds of plants.

4. Before returning to the classroom, be sure students release their animals where they were collected.

Keep an eye out for ant trails so that you'll have an idea of where ant activity is greatest for the next outdoor activity, Tracking Ants.

Back in the Classroom

1. Give students a few minutes to put the finishing touches on their Animal ID Cards.

2. Hold a class discussion of their findings, using the following kinds of questions:

Some teachers recommend that students first write the answers to these questions in their journals and then use their answers as a basis for the class discussion.

- What surprised you?

- Which animal did you find the most of?

- What were the largest animals collected? Smallest? (When a student describes a particular insect, ask everyone who found that kind to raise their hand.)

- Which kind of plant seemed to have the most different kinds of animals? Which kind of plant seemed to have the least kinds of animals? Why do you think there is this difference?

- How did your findings compare with your predictions of where animals would be found? Were they found in the same general places as spiders? How, or in what ways, did moisture, sunlight, and cover seem to make a difference in what animals you found? (Later in the session, when students will add animals to the class map, they can check further to see if there is an overall pattern.)

3. Make some additions to the class list of animals that you made when you introduced this activity.

4. Introduce the concept of *animal communities.* Tell students that an animal community is similar to a human

This discussion may reveal some interesting interactions in the animal communities. Students may have observed evidence of food chains in action, such as ants and spiders feeding on small insects or evidence of animals feeding on plants.

The GEMS guide Terrarium Habitats *gives students an opportunity to explore further the complex interactions of a community of organisms in an ecosystem. Groups of four students study the changes over time in small ecosystems in plastic salad containers.*

If your class map is on a transparency and you are using multiple layers, add the animal symbol with an overhead pen on an "animal" transparency layer.

***The Edge Effect**—Your students may observe that most of the animals live around the edges of the yard, where grass or asphalt meets a border of bushes or trees. While this "edge effect" is more pronounced in a schoolyard, ecologists have also noticed it in other study areas. Ecologists often find the most populous and diverse animal communities are in border areas between two different environments, such as the edge of a forest near a stream or meadow. Animals in these areas can benefit conveniently from the advantages of more than one environment.*

community. An animal community is made up of a variety of different animals that live in the same area and depend on each other for food and other things. Ask students to name several different animals that they found on one plant.

5. Point out that the plant and its animals make up a small community. Some of the animals depend on the plant for food. The plant also provides shelter for animals that feed on the "plant eaters."

6. Invite students to suggest another example of a small community in the schoolyard. Encourage them to be on the lookout for other schoolyard communities of plants and animals.

7. If there is time, go ahead and do the following two classroom follow-up activities now. Otherwise, plan to break here, and do the remaining activities in a separate session.

Recording Locations of Animals on the Class Map

1. Add "Animals" to the key of your large class map, using a different color marker. Have the letter "A" or some other symbol represent all the animals found (except spiders).

2. Tell the students that, while the class is writing in their journals, pairs of students will take turns recording on the class map one place they found an animal on the schoolyard.

3. Give students 10–15 minutes to write and draw in their journals. Meanwhile, call pairs up to the map one at a time.

4. Once the pairs have recorded data on the map, focus the whole class on the map. Ask, "Can you draw any more conclusions by looking at the locations of the animals and spiders found in relation to the environmental factors?" "What about animals and spiders in relation to each other—are spiders in high insect areas?"

Sorting the Animal ID Cards

1. Announce that students will work in teams to sort their ID cards in different ways. Each time they do a sort, they must agree as a group on the characteristic used to separate the cards into groups.

2. Give students an example such as: "If I wanted to sort all of you into two different groups, I might have everyone wearing red move to that corner, and those people not wearing red move to this corner."

3. Ask for examples of ways to group animals. [Spiders/not spiders; brown/black/other are some examples.]

4. Have students form groups of four to six. Distribute the scissors and direct students to cut apart and pool their Animal ID Cards. They should include their spider cards as well as the ones from the shake box activity. If some of the cards show the same kind of animal, they should be stacked together.

5. Ask students to begin sorting their ID cards. Circulate among the groups. Encourage students to agree as a group on one way the animals on the cards can be separated into piles. There is no correct number of piles, as long as their system makes sense to everyone in the group. Say that they need to agree on a reason for their groupings. Encourage groups who have sorted one way, to mix up their cards, and sort them into groups in a different way.

6. When all of the student groups have finished at least one sort, gain the attention of the class, and ask some of them to describe a way they sorted. Tell the class that ecologists work the same way they just did, to put animals into groups, to sort and classify by different characteristics in order to learn more about animals and their relationship to the environment (for example, green insects hiding on a green plant).

7. With older students, you might want to try a *dichotomous* sort, like the ones commonly found in field guides. Have the students first divide their cards into two groups (for example, green/not green or insect/not insect). Then have them choose a new characteristic (like wings/no wings) to divide each subgroup into two more groups, and so on.

8. If the clipboards are needed for another class, have the students keep their maps and ID cards. Then collect the clipboards.

For younger students with little experience in sorting and in using materials cooperatively, you may want to pre-teach sorting with objects like buttons or leaves.

For older students you could take this sort one step further and ask, "What is another characteristic I could use to separate the people wearing red into two groups?"

If some students have finished only one or two ID cards, be sure to team them up with students who have made several cards.

See page 40 for a sample dichotomous key made from sorted Animal ID Cards.

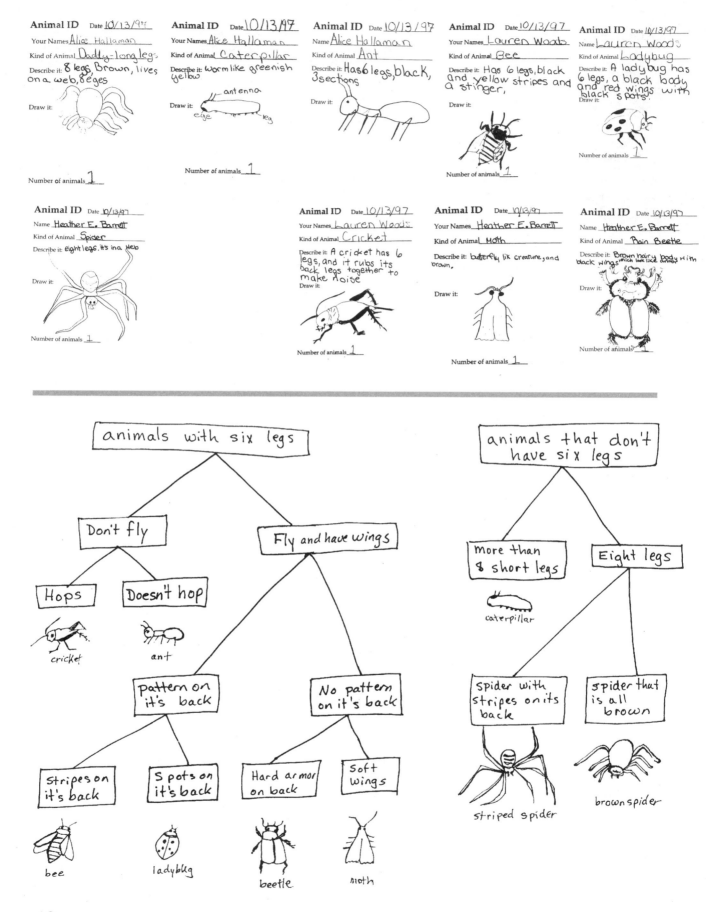

Animal ID Date 10/13/97
Your Names Alice Hallaman
Kind of Animal Daddy-long legs
Describe it: 8 legs, Brown, lives on a web, 8 eyes
Draw it:
Number of animals 1

Animal ID Date 10/13/97
Your Names Alice Hallaman
Kind of Animal Caterpillar
Describe it: worm like greenish yellow
Draw it: antenna eye leg
Number of animals 1

Animal ID Date 10/13/97
Name Alice Hallaman
Kind of Animal Ant
Describe it: Has 6 legs, black, 3 sections
Draw it:

Animal ID Date 10/13/97
Your Names Lauren Woods
Kind of Animal Bee
Describe it: Has 6 legs, black and yellow stripes and a stinger,
Draw it:
Number of animals 1

Animal ID Date 10/13/97
Name Lauren Woods
Kind of Animal Ladybug
Describe it: A ladybug has 6 legs, a black body and red wings with black spots.
Draw it:
Number of animals 1

Animal ID Date 10/13/97
Name Heather E. Barrett
Kind of Animal Spider
Describe it: Eight legs. It's in a Web
Draw it:
Number of animals 1

Animal ID Date 10/13/97
Your Names Lauren Woods
Kind of Animal Cricket
Describe it: A cricket has 6 legs, and it rubs its back legs together to make noise
Draw it:
Number of animals 1

Animal ID Date 10/13/97
Your Names Heather E. Barrett
Kind of Animal Moth
Describe it: butterfly lik creature, and brown,
Draw it:

Animal ID Date 10/13/97
Name Heather E. Barrett
Kind of Animal Rain Beetle
Describe it: Brown hairy body with black wings which look like armor
Draw it:
Number of animals

animals with six legs
Don't fly
Fly and have wings
Hops
Doesn't hop
cricket
ant
Pattern on it's back
No pattern on it's back
Stripes on it's back
Spots on it's back
Hard armor on back
Soft wings
bee
ladybug
beetle
moth

animals that don't have six legs
more than 8 short legs
caterpillar
Eight legs
spider with stripes on its back
spider that is all brown
striped spider
brown spider

Going Further

1. Create a "Schoolyard Animal Guide." Use all of the Animal ID Cards from the whole class to create a bulletin board or a large book. Group the animals according to major categories like "insects" (six legs and three main body parts) and "arachnids" (eight legs and two main body parts).

2. Have students make bar graphs with the ID cards. The class can compile a tally of the total number of each different kind of animal observed.

---

3. Using the Guide to Small Common Schoolyard Animals

Photocopy and staple the Guide to Small Common Schoolyard Animals, found on pages 73–75 for each pair of students. You might begin by having students use the guide to try to identify the animals they described on their Animal ID Cards, and then provide more time outdoors for the class to use the guide to identify more organisms on the schoolyard.

---

*The Guide to Small Common Schoolyard Animals is designed to be used at the end of Activity 3, **after** students have made and classified their own ID cards. This simple guide includes insects and other small animals that are common in most parts of North America. The pages offer some interesting facts, and will help students satisfy some of their natural curiosity about animals they find in the schoolyard and elsewhere. If you wish, you and your students can bring in commercially published field guides too. (Please see the "Resources" section, page 81, for ideas on good field guides to use with students.)*

Activity 4: Tracking Ants

Overview

Ants are found nearly everywhere, and few schools or homes escape their invasions. Their social organization is fascinating and has been the subject of much research. Although many of us view ants as pests, they play an important role in ecosystems. Their tunneling activities add nutrients, air, and water into the soil, enriching it for trees and other plants. Many kinds of ants eat flea larvae, termites, and caterpillars.

This activity usually fits into one class session, but can easily be extended to two. Students work in groups of four, first locating and observing an ant trail (a line of ants) without interfering in any way. Next, they test the responses of ants to barriers, then "displace" an ant and observe how the insect finds its way back. Students also investigate how ants respond to different foods. Results are recorded on a data sheet, and shared in a class discussion. Students record ant trails on their individual maps, but not on the large class map.

As a "Going Further" activity, you may want to challenge your class to discover non-toxic ways to deter ants from invading homes and schools. They can experiment with several substances such as chalk, turmeric, cinnamon, or baking soda that might disrupt the chemical trail or repel ants or both.

What You Need

For the class:
- ❏ the large map of the site (made in Activity 1)
- ❏ 1 cafeteria tray or box lid to carry foods outside
- ❏ 4 types of ant food: 1 tablespoon jelly or jam, a few ounces of apple juice or non-diet soda, a graham cracker, and a small can of cat food
- ❏ 1 sponge (clean and free of soap)
- ❏ 1 ziplock sandwich bag
- ❏ a spoon or popsicle stick
- ❏ grocery bag
- ❏ (optional) a few magnifying lenses

For each group of 4 students:
- ❏ 4–5 flat wooden toothpicks
- ❏ 1 lid (any size—frozen juice can or yogurt container lids are fine)

For each student:
- ❏ clipboard (from Activity 1)
- ❏ pencil
- ❏ 1 student map of study site (made in Activity 1)
- ❏ 1 copy of the Ant Challenges student sheet (master on page 48)
- ❏ a journal

Getting Ready

If you dispense the food too early, you may get an ant invasion in the classroom!

1. Cut the sponge into small pieces, one piece for each group of four students. Put the pieces in a ziplock bag with enough juice or non-diet soda to soak them.

2. Use a spoon or popsicle stick to put small amounts of jelly, graham cracker, and cat food on a lid for each group. Crumble the graham cracker very small so ants can carry it. Add a soaked sponge piece to each lid. Put the lids and toothpicks on a tray.

3. If you haven't already done so, go outside and check the study area to make sure there are some ant trails. If ants are scarce, try putting small dabs of cat food or jelly in various spots a day ahead of time.

4. Make a copy of the Ant Challenges student sheet (master on page 48) for each student.

5. Decide how you'll divide the class into groups of four.

Introducing the Ant Activity

1. Focus the class on the large map of the study area, and ask students where they have seen ants. What were the ants doing?

2. Encourage them to share general experiences with ants. This will probably bring out some of the problems they and their families have had with ants.

3. Point out that ants often come in conflict with people because they are so good at surviving in our environments. In fact they are one of the most successful groups of insects on earth and can be found almost everywhere on land. Let the students know that today their goal as ecologists will be to find out more about ant behavior in the study area.

A word of caution—if the ants around your school include the large red variety, more than one-quarter inch long, caution your students that these ants will bite if touched. Although the bite is tiny and not dangerous, it will sting quite a lot!

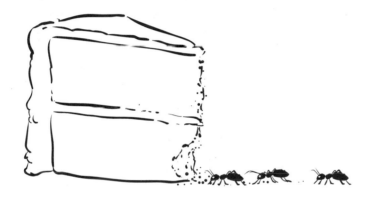

Explaining the Activity

1. Say that the lines of ants they may have seen are called "ant trails." Tell students that they will work in groups of four to find an ant trail to study. The first thing to do will be to mark the location of the ant trail on their maps.

2. Distribute the student sheet, and read the challenges. Explain that, when their group has finished recording their observations for the first three challenges, they can get food samples from you for the fourth challenge.

3. Say that when they get the food, groups should make predictions and decide together which foods to use.

4. Explain that for the fourth challenge they'll use a toothpick to put small amounts of different foods near the ant trail, and then observe what happens. Caution the students not to dump globs of food on top of the ants. Mention that the piece of sponge has been soaked in soda (or

juice) and that they will squeeze very small amounts of juice alongside the ant trail or just place the sponge beside the trail.

5. Assign students to groups of four. If they were collected after Activity 3, distribute the clipboards, and have students attach their Ant Challenges student sheets.

6. Ask students to walk to the study area. Take the tray of ant food, the empty grocery bag (to be used as a garbage bag), and, if you've chosen to use them, a few magnifying lenses to the study area.

Tracking Ants on the Schoolyard

1. Circulate among the groups, noting their observations and reminding every team member to record observations. Ask the following kinds of focusing questions:

- How long is the trail?

- About how many ants are on the trail?

- How do the ants travel along the trail (single file, pairs, groups)?

- Where do the ants seem to be coming from and going to?

- What kinds of things do the ants carry?

- In what ways do the ants touch each other?

2. When groups have finished the first three challenges and recorded observations on the data sheet, let them take toothpicks and a lid of food samples. Remind them to discuss their ideas and develop a plan before just putting food everywhere.

3. Lend assistance if needed. If a group's ant trail is quite long, you may suggest that they divide into pairs and experiment with food at two different spots along the trail.

4. If time and circumstances permit, encourage students to visit the experiments of their colleagues, to see different approaches to the food experiments.

5. Give students a five minute warning to finish and record their experiments. Have a volunteer collect the lids, toothpicks, and sponge pieces in the grocery bag.

Some teachers like to make these questions available for students to take out with them and write answers to in the study site.

Back in the Classroom

1. Give the groups a few minutes to decide what ant behavior they would like to report. They should also choose one person in their group to be the reporter.

2. Give each group a few minutes to share their findings on the various challenges. What new questions did the ant studies bring up?

3. Have students write in their journals. If the clipboards are needed for another class, collect them. Have students keep their maps, Animal ID cards, and Ant Challenges sheets.

Students will probably have recorded some ants on the class map as part of the shake box activity. Adding more data to the class map is optional during the ant activities.

Going Further

1. Ant Deterrents. People all over the world are interested in ways to discourage ants from taking over human homes. You might try the following activity with the whole class, or make it available as a special project for selected students. Invite students to experiment to discover non-toxic ways to deter ants from invading home or school. One possible ant deterrent they might try is regular chalkboard chalk. Some others might be common cooking ingredients such as cinnamon, turmeric, and baking soda. Have students check with their parents before using these or any other household substances. Ask students to place small amounts of different substances on an ant trail and observe the ants' behavior over the next day or so. Have the student scientists describe in writing how they conducted their experiments, the outcome, and recommendations for future experiments and applications.

2. Continued Observations. If possible, have the students revisit their ant trails later in the day or over the next several days. Sometimes the results of the food experiments are more conclusive after some time has passed. (For example, one food is gone, another is all still there.)

3. Ant Anatomy. Use the drawing on page 49 to review the main body parts of the ant (and all insects)—head, thorax, abdomen, six legs, etc.

Name _____

Ant Challenges

1. **Observe:** Watch an ant trail. (Don't disturb the ants.) What do you see?

2. **Road Block:** Gently put something across the ant trail. What do the ants do?

3. **Take Away:** Carefully use a leaf or stick to move one ant a few feet away from the ant trail. What does the ant do?

4. **Food Tests:** Put a small amount of food near the ant trail. Watch for a while. What happens?

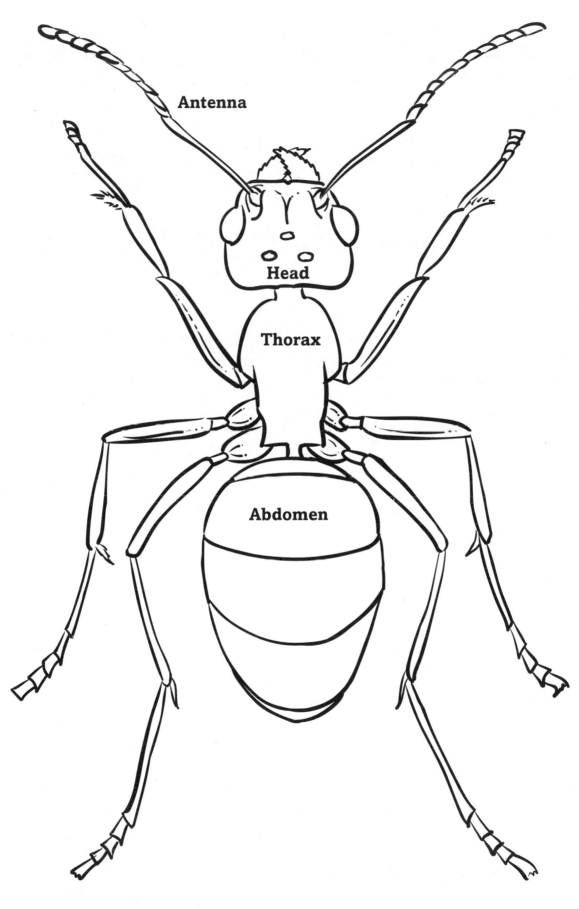

Antenna

Head

Thorax

Abdomen

Activity 5: Special Study Sites

Overview

When ecologists study an ecosystem, they usually don't have the time and resources to study everything in the total area, so they select small areas to study closely. These small areas are called *sample study sites.* Ecologists try to sample all of the different kinds of communities in the ecosystem to find out what the different organisms require to survive.

By now, having surveyed the environmental factors of the study area and the life within it, students are ready to choose a particular spot to investigate in depth. In this activity, students may work singly or in pairs. They select a site that is of interest to them, use a string loop to define their site, and mark the location on their maps. They carefully observe and describe their area, the environmental factors, and any plants and animals located there.

Special study sites provide a compelling stepping stone for students to pursue their natural curiosity about the environment. Imagine the ecological wisdom and interest that could develop at a school as students discover and follow the variety of life inhabiting their outdoor laboratory. We hope these techniques for studying nature generate a wealth of student-directed investigations and projects.

What You Need

For the class:
- ❑ the large map of the site (made in Activity 1)
- ❑ a selection of wide-tipped, colored felt markers
- ❑ a few magnifying lenses
- ❑ about 100 yards of string or yarn to make loops

For each student:
- ❑ clipboard (from Activity 1)
- ❑ pencil
- ❑ 1 student map of study site (made in Activity 1)
- ❑ a string loop*
- ❑ a small piece of cardboard or a stick (to wrap string around)
- ❑ 1 piece of white unlined paper
- ❑ 1 piece of white lined paper

❑ a journal
❑ (*optional*) a page of Animal ID Cards (master on page 30)
❑ (*optional*) a paper or plastic bag or newspaper to sit on at study site

*If your study area isn't large or varied enough for each student to have a study site, consider having students work in teams of two. In this case you'll need only half as many string loops.

Getting Ready

1. Some teachers find that there is plenty of space and variety on their schoolyards for each student to choose a study site. However, if your space is limited, you may decide to have students work in pairs or even groups of three or four for this activity.

2. For each string loop, cut a three-yard length of string and tie the ends. Wind each string loop around a piece of cardboard or a stick so it won't get tangled. Leave one string loop unwound for your demonstration.

3. If you choose to use them, duplicate a page of Animal ID Cards (master on page 30) for each student, plus a few extra.

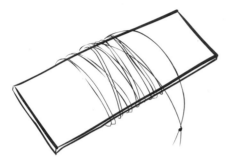

To save yourself preparation time, you may want to distribute pre-cut pieces of string to students at the beginning of the activity and have them tie and wrap their own loops.

Introducing the Activity

1. Let the students know that today they will each get to use their skills as ecologists to study a smaller site in the schoolyard study area.

2. Hold up a string loop. Explain that their personal study site will be the area within the loop. Of course, they can adjust the shape of their string to include as many interesting things as possible.

Although it may be more possible inside the classroom to keep attention focused and for all students to hear, many teachers prefer to model the loop procedure outside. This is absolutely fine.

3. Model the procedure in the classroom. Arrange a string loop on a table. Ask the class to imagine that the tabletop is a place you've chosen on the schoolyard. Say that once they choose where their loop will go, they'll mark its location on their maps.

4. Say that they'll get a piece of unlined paper to draw their personal site. On the chalkboard, draw a shape like that of your string loop. Read the following sample description of a study site as you draw and label a small spider, a leaf, and a few pebbles.

My Study Site Up Close

My study site is hot, with no damp places and hardly any shade. The only shade or cover is under all the dry, warm clods of dirt. These chunks of dirt are all different sizes, with little sticks and dead grass sticking out of them. And there's one brown, dusty rock shaped like a tiny bicycle seat.

A brown spider about as big around as a pencil races out from under one dirt clod. It goes about four inches in one second and is out of sight under another hunk of dirt. I wonder where it makes its home.

I see one white, curled up, dead roly-poly, with little, pale mummy legs neatly folded into the curve of the shell. Some pieces of dried grass wave a bit in the breeze.

One dirt clod is sparkling in the sun like someone sprinkled glitter on it. On looking closer, I see it's not glitter, but some sort of slime! Maybe a snail or slug crawled by this morning when things were a little cooler and wetter.

5. Remind the students about the environmental factors from Activity 1 (sunlight, moisture, cover, etc.). Say that after observing their special study site, they'll write, on lined paper, every detail they can about the environmental factors in their site, as well as any animals or plants they observe.

6. Point out that in the previous activities, they were moving around the schoolyard, but this time they'll need to stay in one place and focus on it for about 20 minutes. If you're using them, show the bags or newspapers, and say that if the ground is wet, they can use them to sit on.

7. Distribute the unlined and lined paper, string loops, pencils, bags or newspapers to sit on (optional), and, if they were collected after Activity 4, the clipboards. Have students add the paper to their clipboards. Ask the students to walk to the study area and select their personal site. Take along a few magnifying lenses.

On the Schoolyard

1. As students choose their spots, place their strings, and settle down to focus, go around and remind them to mark the location of their study site on their map, then observe and record carefully.

2. Circulate among the students, offering Animal ID Cards and magnifying lenses to assist with observations.

3. When everyone has finished, signal the students to rewind their string loops and take everything back to the classroom.

Back in the Classroom

1. Ask students to share some of their discoveries.

2. Ask students to reflect on why they found (or didn't find) animals in their site, given the environmental conditions. Encourage them to suggest what factors (cover, moisture, etc.) might be influencing the plants and animals.

3. Ask students to raise their hands if they chose sites with lots of cover. Ask how many found animals there. Ask the same questions for very open sites. Which sites had the most animals?

4. Ask students to think about how their personal site might change over the next few months (or years), and write about it in their journals. Have them try to predict how changes in the environment might affect the number and kinds of plants and animals at the site.

5. Consider using some of the "Going Further" suggestions below to extend students' explorations of their study sites, encourage deeper analysis of the ecology of the schoolyard, or to connect students' studies to art, literature, and music.

Going Further

1. Ask each student to create an ingredient list or recipe for their special study site. They can use their notes and drawings to help them remember. Ask them to be sure the recipe includes plants, soil, and climate as well as animals. For example:

1	square foot of medium brown soil
14	gray speckled rocks, some sprinkled with moss
3	bushes
1	pine tree with sap dripping down
6	weeds
32	ants
6	black crawly bugs
2	flies
1	spider
1	broken spider web

Mix well with
1	cup of moisture
2	dashes of sunlight

Serves…me!

2. Going Further with the Class Map. Conduct a "Map Analysis Session" in which groups interpret various sets of data such as: identifying the most favorable areas for spiders, ants, and other animals; comparing numbers of animals along edges to numbers in the open; comparing animal numbers found in wet versus dry areas, sunny versus shady, or cover versus open; identifying communities of plants and animals. Invite students to continue adding information to the map as they continue their individual studies. Tell students that the map will be saved to compare with future studies by students.

3. Have each student come up with a combination of several environmental factors (such as, high moisture, low light, low cover). Ask them to create an imaginary animal that is adapted to these particular environmental conditions. They should include what it eats, how it prevents itself from being eaten (hiding and camouflage count as well as poisonous bites!), and how it lives (alone like spiders, in groups like ants, or in other ways). Have the students draw and describe their new animal, being sure to label all parts.

4. Have students try to find each other's study sites using only the description.

Many of these "Going Further" activities make effective assessment pieces.

You may want to read some or all of the excerpt from Annie Dillard's Pilgrim at Tinker Creek *that we include immediately following this activity. We also provide brief writings from conservationists, such as John Muir and Rachel Carson.*

5. Invite students to use shake boxes or ant food at their own study sites.

6. Encourage students to visit their study sites over the school year to observe seasonal changes.

7. Invite students to develop a collaborative project to improve the schoolyard environment.

8. Ask students to observe birds that visit the schoolyard. Put out feeders to increase the numbers and kinds of birds.

9. Choose a selection of nature writings to read in conjunction with art or creative writing activities. Have students write descriptions and/or poetry about their special spots, with illustrations, if the students are inclined. Create a "For the Love of Nature" corner to display their efforts. This could be broadened to look at art, literature, music, or sculpture inspired by nature.

A Quick Stop at Tinker Creek

I am sitting under a sycamore by Tinker Creek. I am really here, alive on the intricate earth under trees. But under me, directly under the weight of my body on the grass, are other creatures, just as real, for whom also this moment, this tree, is "it." Take just the top inch of soil, the world squirming right under my palms. In the top inch of forest soil, biologists found "an average of 1,356 living creatures present in each square foot, including 865 mites, 265 springtails, 22 millipedes, 19 adult beetles and various members of 12 other forms… Had an estimate also been made of the microscopic population, it might have ranged up to two billion bacteria and many millions of fungi, protozoa and algae—in a mere *teaspoonful* of soil." The chrysalids of butterflies linger here too, folded, rigid, and dreamless. I might as well include these creatures in this moment, as best I can…

Earthworms in staggering procession lurch through the grit underfoot, gobbling downed leaves and spewing forth castings by the ton. Moles mine intricate tunnels in networks; there are often so many of these mole tunnels here by the creek that when I walk, every step is a letdown. A mole is almost entirely loose inside its skin, and enormously mighty. If you can catch a mole, it will, in addition to biting you memorably, leap from your hand in a single convulsive contraction and be gone as soon as you have it. You are never really able to see it; you only feel its surge and thrust against your palm, as if you hold a beating heart in a paper bag. What could I not do if I had the power and will of a mole! But the mole churns earth…

Under my spine, the sycamore roots suck watery salts. Root tips thrust and squirm between particles of soil, probing minutely; from their roving, burgeoning tissues spring infinitesimal root hairs, transparent and hollow, which affix themselves to specks of grit and sip… Under the world's conifers—under the creekside cedar behind where I sit—a mantle of fungus wraps the soil in a weft, shooting out blind thread after frail thread of palest dissolved white. From root tip to root tip, root hair to root hair, these filaments loop and wind; the thought of them always reminds me of Rimbaud's "I have stretched cords from steeple to steeple, garlands from window to window, chains of gold from star to star, and I dance."… Here the very looped soil is an intricate throng of praise. Make connections; let rip; and dance where you can.

—Annie Dillard
Pilgrim at Tinker Creek

…In a dry, hot, monotonous forested plateau, seemingly boundless, you come suddenly and without warning upon the abrupt edge of a gigantic sunken landscape of the wildest, most multitudinous features, and those features, sharp and angular, are made out of flat beds of limestone and sandstone forming a spiry, jagged, gloriously colored mountain range countersunk in a level gray plain. It is a hard job to sketch it even in scrawniest outline; and, try as I may, not in the least sparing myself, I cannot tell the hundredth part of the wonders of its features—the side canyons, gorges, alcoves, cloisters, and amphitheaters of vast sweep and depth, carved in its magnificent walls; the throng of great architectural rocks it contains resembling castles, cathedrals, temples, and palaces, towered and spired and painted, some of them nearly a mile high, yet beneath one's feet.

… All the canyon rock-beds are lavishly painted, except a few neutral bars and the granite notch at the bottom occupied by the river, which makes but little sign. It is a vast wilderness of rocks in a sea of light, colored and glowing like oak and maple woods in autumn, when the sun-gold is richest.

…the COLORS, the living rejoicing COLORS, chanting morning and evening in chorus to heaven! Whose brush or pencil, however lovingly inspired, can give us these? And if paint is of no effect, what hope lies in pen-work? Only this: some may be incited by it to go and see for them-selves.

—John Muir
Steep Trails
Chapter 24 :
The Grand Canyon of the Colorado

The mud flats were strewn with the shells of that small, exquisitely colored mollusk, the rose tellin, looking like scattered petals of pink roses. There must have been a colony nearby, living buried just under the surface of the mud. At first the only creature visible was a small heron in gray and rusty plumage—a reddish egret that waded across the flat with the stealthy, hesitant movements of its kind. But other land creatures had been there, for a line of fresh tracks wound in and out among the mangrove roots, marking the path of a raccoon feeding on the oysters that gripped the supporting roots with projections from their shells. Soon I found the tracks of a shore bird, probably a sanderling, and followed them a little; then they turned toward the water and were lost, for the tide had erased them and made them as though they had never been.

—Rachel Carson
The Edge of the Sea

Behind the Scenes

Ecology and Ecosystem

As evident from the title and noted in the text, through this unit your students become conversant with aspects of *ecology* to guide their investigations. The word ecology comes from the ancient Greek language—*eco* for house and *ology* which means to study. In recent decades, with the intensely increased environmental awareness worldwide, most of us have become more familiar with terms like ecology and ecosystem which are often used by scholars, scientists, researchers, and environmentalists. *Ecosystem,* as the name implies, is a term given to any place or habitat in which a number of organisms (plants and/or animals) live. Naturalists who study the vast array of ecosystems large and small on our planet have uncovered many systems of complex interconnections and interdependencies.

An ecosystem can be made up of many different plant and animal communities, each with its own distinct kinds of organisms that depend on each other for food, shelter, and other special needs. Some examples of common schoolyard plant communities include: lawn, ivy, tall grass and weeds, conifer shrubs, and deciduous shrubs and trees. Animals often rely on several plant communities. For example, some birds find their food in grassy communities, but also need shrub or tree communities for nesting and roosting.

As your students discover through the activities, when ecologists study an ecosystem, they usually don't have the time and resources to study everything in the total area, so they select small areas to study closely. These small areas are called *sample study sites.* Ecologists try to sample all of the different kinds of communities in the ecosystem to find out what the different organisms require to survive.

Communities of Organisms

Plants and animals live in certain places because environmental factors are suitable for their life cycles. Environmental factors that affect the organisms living in an area include: temperature, light, moisture, soil type and available minerals, wind, other plants and animals, and the impact of people.

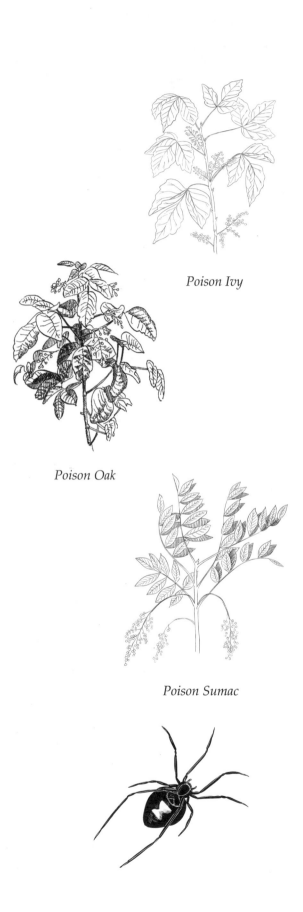

Poison Ivy

Poison Oak

Poison Sumac

A ***community*** is a group of plants and animals that live together in an area. Some communities, such as the community of organisms in Lake Michigan, are huge. Other communities—such as those found on a pine tree, oak tree, or in a hedge—are composed of fewer organisms and occupy much less space. Whatever the size and makeup of a community, certain factors are universal. All communities contain plants that make food to support the community. Some of the animals in the community eat the plants. Many communities also contain predatory animals that eat other animals. In addition, most communities contain fungi and microorganisms that decompose the community's dead organisms and waste products. The decomposers return minerals and nutrients to the environment where they can be reused by the community of plants and animals.

The plants around the schoolyard will provide clues about the variety of animals living in this small community. Spiders leave their webs and small animals such as caterpillars and grasshoppers leave munch marks on the leaves. Many different kinds of insects attack almost every part of every kind of plant. The part of the plant insects most frequently nibble is the leaf. Evidence left in the wake of feeding insects is quite varied. Some chew small round holes in leaves, and others make worm-shaped channels. As students sample the vegetation of the schoolyard for small animals, they may well find fascinating evidence of animals at work: galls, spittle bug foam, caterpillar tents, and curled-up leaves.

Checking the Schoolyard for Potential Hazards

Be on the lookout for potentially dangerous trash, such as discarded needles and broken glass, as well as plants and animals that may cause allergic reactions or dangerous bites. If you discover a hazard, such as a patch of poison ivy, poison oak, or a yellow jacket nest, flag or mark the area as a warning to students, and alert your principal and the school gardener. If there are wood piles or areas of debris that might harbor snakes and poisonous spiders, mark or flag these as "out-of-bounds" for investigations.

Black Widow Spiders

The undersides of playground equipment, woodpiles, and dark dry shelters are the most common schoolyard hangouts for these spiders. We suggest that you recruit the help of the school gardener to check areas of the yard, and to exterminate black widows in frequently used play structures. We recommend that great care and moderation be used during any extermination effort, in order to protect the many small but beneficial schoolyard animals, including predators of black widows such as other spiders, deer mice, and birds.

This spider is common throughout the country, but due to its reclusive and non-aggressive behavior, fewer than 500 people are bitten each year, and 96% survive. The males and tiny spiderlings are harmless, but a bite from a female with its round, glossy, black abdomen requires immediate medical attention. The black widow spider venom is a potentially deadly neurotoxin that causes paralysis of the breathing muscles.

Female spiders often hang upside down in the web with the under side of their abdomen showing the characteristic red hour-glass pattern. If you find a black widow spider out on her web, take the opportunity to teach children to recognize and to avoid it.

Brown Recluse or Violin Spider

This spider, found from Kansas and Missouri south to Texas and west to California, lives in schoolyard haunts similar to those of the black widow spider. It prefers dry dark sheltered areas among debris, but will also crawl into discarded clothing. It is a relatively small spider (6–11 mm in length), with a loose and irregular web, and is often called the violin spider because of the fiddle shape on the top of the head (cephalothorax). People bitten by this spider find that the wounds are very slow to heal, forming a crust and then a deep crater that persists for months. If you suspect you have brown recluse spiders at your site, we recommend that you contact your local health department for assistance with identification.

Tick Avoidance

Reported cases of tick-borne diseases, such as Lyme Disease, in people have been increasing in most regions of the country, as doctors and the public become more knowledgeable about the symptoms, the diseases, and the ticks that transmit them. If your schoolyard includes, or is adjacent to, large areas of woodland or tall grass interspersed with bushes, precautions such as the following should be taken to avoid ticks.

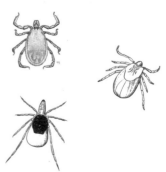

- Before the day of the investigations, direct children to wear closed shoes, long pants, long-sleeved shirts, and light-colored clothing so ticks can easily be seen.

- Tuck pant legs into boots or socks, and tuck shirts into pants.

- Apply insect repellent containing permethrin to pants, socks, and shoes.

- Check yourself and your students for ticks hourly and after the activity.

- Carry fine-tipped tweezers, an alcohol swab, and a sandwich-size, ziplock, plastic bag with you.

What to do if a Tick is Found

If a tick is found walking on a student, use tweezers or a tissue to place the tick in a plastic bag. **Save the tick for identification.**

If a tick has bitten a student, prompt removal may prevent disease transmission.

Use tweezers or tissue to protect the fingers when you remove the tick. If the tick is squeezed with fingers, diseases may be forced into the wound.

Grasp the tick's mouth parts as close to the skin as possible and gently pull the tick straight out, steadily and firmly. Do not twist or jerk the tick. Never apply chemicals to the tick or use lit matches, as the tick may regurgitate bacteria into the wound.

Wash hands and the bite site with soap and water, and apply antiseptic to the bite site.

Always save the tick for identification! To keep the tick alive to be tested for Lyme Disease, add a few stalks of green grass to the plastic bag. To find out where ticks may be sent for testing, call your local Vector Control, Mosquito Abatement District, or county health department.

Notify the student's parent of the tick bite, and recommend that they report the bite to their doctor.

Resources and Information about Ticks

The Rhode Island Tick Pickers
University of Rhode Island
Tick Research Lab at the Biological Sciences Dept.
100 Flagg Road
Kingston, RI 02881
(401) 874-2650
e-mail: [ticklab@uriacc.uri.edu]
http://www.uri.edu/artsci/zool/ticklab/Ticks.html

Ticks and What You Can Do About Them, Roger Drummond, Wilderness Press, Berkeley, California, 1990.

The Lyme Times is a publication of articles and research summaries produced bi-monthly by the Lyme Disease Resource Center, P.O. Box 1891, Sonoma, CA 95476.

"Lyme Disease: The Facts, the Challenge," in *Lyme Disease Booklet*, NIAMS/NIH, 1 AMS Circle, Bethesda, MD 20892
http://www.nih.gov/niams/healthinfo/lyme/

Lyme Disease at KidSource Online
http://205.164.116.200/kidsource/content/lymedis.html

Spiders

Most of us are familiar with the cobwebs that often adorn corners of houses, garages, or patios. Broom in hand, we brush the sticky threads away, only to find that they have reappeared a few days later. These webs are the skillful work of small, eight-legged predators—spiders. Spiders make their own silk and weave it into traps to catch insects and other small animals for food. Most spiders are active mainly at night, spending the daylight hours out of sight near their webs.

The spider webs you and your students find will generally belong to females. Most male spiders do not weave webs but build nests near a female's web. If you look closely, sometimes you can find the much smaller male in the female's web where they get much of their food. Because many spiders will eat their own species, spider mating often involves elaborate strategies used by the often smaller male spider to prevent the female from dining on him, at least until after they have mated.

Webs are spun from silk, which the web weaver produces in specialized glands. She releases the silk through openings called spinnerets near the end of her abdomen and handles the silk with tiny claws on the ends of her legs. She may produce more than one kind of silk. Different sizes, textures, and strengths of silk threads are often needed for different purposes, such as catching prey (sticky silk), building web-foundation lines (non-sticky threads), making nests, spinning egg cocoons, and "ballooning," which is riding air currents at the end of a free-floating thread of silk. Most spiders leave a dragline of silk wherever they go, which helps prevent them from falling. They periodically attach the dragline to the substrate (a leaf, the ground, etc.) with tiny silk attachment discs. These discs can be seen easily against glass, if you leave a spider in a glass jar for a while.

Each distinctive type of web is made by a different kind of spider. Please also see the spider web key following Session 2 in this guide. There are funnel webs, sheet webs, triangle webs, globe webs, orb webs, and irregular cobwebs. When an insect lands in a web, the spider feels— with its legs—the vibrations the insect makes and quickly moves to the struggling prey. Many spiders bind their prey with silk. Spiders bite their prey to inject a paralyzing poison. Juices from digestive glands injected into the prey liquefy the insect's body, and the spider sucks the liquid into its mouth.

We know that web-building spiders produce sticky and non-sticky silk. We do not know for certain what keeps a spider from sticking to its own web, but one explanation is that the spider walks primarily on the non-sticky threads. Specialized claws enable web spiders to grasp and walk on web threads. However, one kind of spider will stick to the web of another kind of spider.

Not all spiders build webs to catch their prey. Some quietly stalk and then grab their prey, while others camouflage themselves in a flower and wait for an unsuspecting insect to visit the flower.

Spider Safety

Although most spiders cannot harm humans, you should caution the youngsters against handling them. There is one poisonous web spider the students can easily identify and avoid: the Black Widow. This spider has a rounded, glossy black body with an hourglass-shaped red or orange mark on the underside of its body. The shape of this mark varies from spider to spider, and some black widow spiders may have more than one mark.

Finding Webs

Many spiders are dormant during the winter, so you will have better luck with these activities at other times of year. Also, rain destroys webs, so wait a day after a rain before hunting for webs outdoors. A good time to look for webs is just after dew or fog, as the sparking drops help make the webs more visible. Spiders and webs are everywhere: on buildings, in pipes, on fences, hedges, bushes, trees, and under outdoor light fixtures.

Amazing Spider Facts

Spider Numbers

15	Number of minutes one kind of Brazilian spider can stay under water.
20	Number of species of spiders that are poisonous enough to harm people. Only three of them—the black widow, brown recluse, and hobo spider—live in North America.
30	Number of years some large female spiders can live.
40	Number of times its own length a jumping spider can leap. If you could jump like that, you'd cover about 160 feet (48 m) in one bound.
25,000	Number of feet high some baby spiders can float in the air. That's as high as some airplanes fly.
35,000	Number of species of spiders that scientists have identified so far.
110,000	Number of spider species that scientists think exist.
2,000,000	Number of spiders that may live in an area the size of a football field.

- Spider blood may surprise you. Instead of being red, it's pale blue.

- Spiders taste with their feet.

- Web builders have three claws on each foot. The middle claw hooks over the silk threads of their webs.

- Cobweb weavers have special "teeth" on their back legs to comb their silk. This makes the silk look soft and fluffy. It also makes tiny loops in the silk that can trip insects and tangle them up.

- Baby web builders climb up to the top of a blade of grass or onto a branch and let out a few threads of silk to catch the wind and become airborne. They can travel hundreds of miles this way.

- The Water Spider builds a web underwater that looks like a dome. It carries air bubbles from the surface to fill its dome with air. It can feed, mate, and raise a family inside the dome of air!

- A mother Wolf Spider carries her babies on her back for about a week after they hatch. She can carry hundreds of little spiderlings this way.

- Wolf Spiders shed their exoskeletons about 12 times before they are completely grown.

- According to an ancient Navajo legend, the technique for weaving their beautiful blankets was taught to a young girl in their tribe by Spider Woman. The girl wandered away from her village one day and found a big hole in the ground. Peeking inside, she looked into the home of Spider Woman who was sitting at her loom weaving a blanket. Spider Woman welcomed the girl and taught her the secrets of weaving which the girl passed on to her people.

- The word "arachnid" comes from the Greek *Arachne,* the name of a woman whose weavings were the most beautiful in all of Greece. Because she claimed her weavings were more beautiful than those of the goddess Athena, she was turned into a spider and the cloth Arachne was weaving became her web.

Ants

Variety

At any one time, it is estimated that at least 1 quadrillion ants are alive on earth. There are at least 10,000 different kinds of ants, and these insects—which are related to bees and wasps—have been around for more than 100 million years. While the homes of ants are often diverse, most live in nests in the ground, wood, or in natural cavities. However, some notable exceptions include the weaver ants of Africa, Asia, and Australia that live in trees and weave leaves to make nests. The army ants of South America and the driver ants of Africa have no permanent nests—on the move most of the time, these ants carry their young with them as they search the countryside for food.

The feeding behaviors of ants also vary greatly. The leaf-cutter ants of South and Central America cut leaves to use as compost for growing a special kind of fungus, which they eat. The harvester ants collect and store grain for food. The honey pot ants use their bodies to store nectar, which nourishes the ant community when food is scarce. The common, brown garden ant eats scraps of food from our houses as well as dead insects, juice from aphids, nectar from flowers and juice from stems, seeds, and mushrooms. It digs tunnels and chambers in the earth to build its home. The ant piles the dirt, which it removes from its tunnels, in a neat mound at the entrance. Other mound builders are the harvester ants, small yellow meadow ants, and wood ants.

Body Structure of Queen, Male, and Worker Ants

Ants, like other insects, have bodies that are divided into three main parts: a head, a thorax, and an abdomen. Ants have six legs, two antennae, and two compound eyes. Some ants also have three simple eyes, called *ocelli,* which are sensitive to light and dark. Ants have two claws on each foot, which they use to dig, climb, and fight. Male ants and young queens have four wings. The two antennae on the front of the ant's head are slender, jointed feelers used for smelling and touching, and possibly for hearing. The antennae are vital to an ant since its sense of smell helps it find food, recognize danger, and identify other members of its colony. Ants also have a special stomach called a *crop* (sometimes called a "social stomach"). When worker ants collect food, they carry it back to the nest in these stomachs. They then regurgitate the food to feed other members of the colony. They can store food in their crops for long periods of time to distribute when needed.

Ant Sizes

Different species of ants range in size from the small brown garden ant to the 1 ½" long bulldog ant of Australia. Queens, males, and workers within a species are different sizes. The queens are the largest ants in a colony, and the workers are the smallest. Sometimes the size of the workers in a colony will vary depending on the job the worker does. The smaller worker has jobs such as cleaning and feeding other ants; the larger worker has more aggressive roles such as guarding the anthill.

Ant Life Span

The queen ant lives considerably longer than the female worker or the male. A queen may live 20 years or more. One brown garden ant queen lived 29 years in captivity. A worker may live as many as seven years—and a male dies immediately after its mating flight. An anthill may outlast a human lifetime.

Ant Society

All ants are social, living in colonies with one or more queens, female workers, winged males, and winged young queens. The colonies, which often contain upwards of 20 million individuals, are predominantly female. The males and young queens need wings for their nuptial flight, during which the males fertilize the young queens. A queen ant only needs to be fertilized once in her lifetime. Once fertilized, a young queen loses her wings and begins her lifelong job of laying eggs. Since a male ant's only job is fertilization, he dies soon after mating. Female workers do a variety of jobs: dig tunnels and chambers to build a nest, clean and repair the nest, care for the queens and young, and defend the anthill. They also leave the nest to collect food to share with all the members of the ant community.

Metamorphosis and Diet

When a queen ant mates, she stores millions of live sperm cells in a pouch in her abdomen. After mating, the queen begins laying eggs. Some worker ants feed and clean the queen. Others, commonly called nurse ants, take the eggs from the queen and put them in nurseries. The eggs hatch into white, worm-like creatures called larvae. The nurse ants feed the larvae and lick the eggs and larvae to clean them. The saliva makes the eggs or larvae stick together in clumps, making them easier for the nurse ants to move when the chambers get too hot, too cold, or too wet. The food that the workers feed to the larvae depends on the species. Some ants feed regurgitated liquids to their young, harvester ants feed seed parts to their larvae, and army ants feed insect parts to their larvae. Queen, male, and worker larvae all look alike at first. As they grow, some become much fatter than others. The largest larvae become queens, the middle-size ones become males, and the smallest become female workers. After about 15–30 days, the larvae use silk, secreted from glands near their mouths, to spin cocoons. Some ant larvae species do not build cocoons; their tough skin provides enough protection. Inside their cocoons or skins, the larvae change to pupae. The pupae, over a period of 13–22 days, develop into adult ants. The nurse ants help the young adults, which are white and somewhat transparent at first, emerge from their encasements. This change from egg to adult, called *metamorphosis*, takes about 87 days.

Scent Trail

An ant becomes excited when it finds food. On its way back to its nest, it dabs the end of its abdomen on the ground, leaving chemical substances called *pheromones*. These chemicals produce a scent. Other ants from the nest follow the scent to the food, leaving more scent on the trail as they carry food back to the nest. When there is no more food left, the ants stop producing pheromones, and the scent trail goes away in a few minutes.

Ant Enemies

Ants have many enemies, such as birds, frogs, toads, lizards, spiders, anteaters, as well as other insects and other kinds of ants. People kill ants by stepping on them and spraying them with insecticides. Red ants often attack anthills of black ants to steal the cocoons. The black ants that hatch from these cocoons become the slaves of the red ants. As a defense, ants bite and sting. Some ants spray a chemical from the tips of their abdomens as a warning when they detect danger. Sometimes after biting an enemy, an ant will spray chemicals into the open wound.

Amazing Ant Facts

- Most ants have two compound eyes—each eye is made up of from 6 to 1,000 tiny individual eyes.

- There are about 10,000 different species of ants, some as big as 2 ½ inches (75 cm).

- Ant antennae have 9 to 13 tiny joints and detect flavors, sounds, and odors.

- A queen ant may live from 5 to 15 years and will lay thousands of eggs during that time.

- An ant hill in Africa was reported to be 25 feet (7.5 meters) tall!

- Most ants are black or brown. One kind, found in the tropics, is green.

- Harvester ants store seeds in chambers in their nests. One nest in Arizona had 436 chambers with 12,358 ants in the colony.

- One red ant colony had 238,000 members.

- The common red wood ant eats insects—many of them are garden pests. The ants in one nest brought in 28 insects in a minute. At this rate, this colony could capture 10,000 insects in a day.

- Army ants stream through the jungle in large numbers. Usually the marching columns are about five ants wide. They travel at a rate of a hundred feet an hour. A colony moves through the jungle for 17 days, stopping each night, then moving on again. At the end of the 17-day period they stop and establish a temporary nest while the huge queen produces nearly 30,000 eggs.

- Some soldier ants use their enlarged head to plug the entrance to their nest to keep out enemies.

- Leaf cutter ants from Louisiana and Texas to Central America don't eat the leaves they cut, they eat fungus. They use the leaves to nourish the fungus that is grown in their nests.

- Many ants keep a "herd" of aphids and "milk" sweet juices from them. The Acrobatic ants actually build a "barn" to house their aphid "cattle."

Guide to Small Common Schoolyard Animals

Ants
You can easily see the three main body parts of this common insect—head, thorax, and abdomen. During warm weather you might find ants with wings, as they mate and travel to start a new colony. Ant colonies usually have thousands of workers and guard ants, so if you find one ant there are certain to be many more. *Follow an ant trail back to the colony.*

Aphids
These tiny, round, soft-bodied insects suck plant juices for food. Aphids have wings at certain times of the year. Usually green, aphids can also be black or brown, and may be tended by ants that "milk" the aphids to get the sweet plant juices. *If you find aphids, look for worker ants visiting and tending the "farm."*

Bees, Yellow Jackets, and Small (non-stinging) Wasps
Honeybees and bumblebees normally will not bother quiet observers unless their hive or nest is disturbed. Beware of aggressive yellow jackets; they will sting if you swat at them. If you find one of their gray paper nests, avoid it and immediately tell your teacher.

There are many species of small, harmless, narrow-waisted wasps that can be found in vegetation around buildings. Many are parasites of other insects, and help reduce the numbers of plant-eaters such as caterpillars. Some insert their eggs into a leaf or twig, creating a gall or growth on the plant that protects the growing larvae. *If you find several galls, ask your teacher's help in opening one.*

Beetles
Many interesting kinds of beetles can be found around schoolyards. They are all hard-bodied and many have spectacular colors and designs. They have two pairs of wings, but the top wings form an armor-like shell over the soft, inner flying wings. Some beetles are predators, some eat plants, and others are scavengers. *There are more than 30,000 different kinds of beetles in North America. How many different kinds of beetles can you find?*

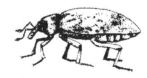

Bugs—these are True Bugs!
This large group of insects resemble flattened beetles and come in many beautiful colors and sizes. The wings fold flat across the back usually forming an "X" pattern. They have sucking/piercing mouth parts that look like a small straw under the head. *Use a magnifier to examine how the upper wings are half leathery and half membranous.*

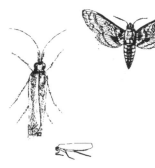

Butterflies and Moths

These have four large wings that are covered with tiny iridescent scales. Many of their larvae, or caterpillars, are well camouflaged as they munch on leaves. **Some have stinging spines and itchy hairs, so just look—don't touch.** Most moths are active at night and hide in vegetation during the day. The common Lawn Moth has slender wings that are usually folded against its body when at rest. The tiny caterpillars of these moths feed on stems or roots of grass. *If you find a caterpillar, look for its six legs near the head that will become its adult legs. How many other "larvae legs" does it have?*

Centipedes

Don't pick up these fast moving, worm-like animals—they can sting and bite! The many-legged centipedes hide under leaves and logs and prey on small soil animals. They are crustaceans, and have two large antennae and two large sensors at their back end.

Earthworms

Earthworms are segmented and have a light-colored band around the body about one-third of the way down the body, near the head. They feed on decaying plants, and are a very important soil builder. *Look for earthworms after a rain, crawling across walkways. Once you have observed them, return them to the safety of some leaf litter or a lawn.*

Earwigs

Earwigs hide during the day under leaves and debris, then come out at night to feed on dead leaves, fruits, and petals. The females protect their eggs and feed their nymphs until they are strong enough to find their own food. *Earwigs don't go in people's ears, but how do you think they might have gotten their name? Find out more about earwigs at your library.*

Flies, Gnats, Mosquitoes, and Craneflies

Flies have only one pair of transparent wings. Many fly larvae feed on decaying vegetation and mushrooms in the soil, recycling Nature's waste. *Use a magnifier to locate the tiny knobs (halteres) behind the wings that may indicate that fly ancestors had two pairs of wings.*

Grasshoppers and Crickets

These long-legged jumpers come in many sizes and shapes, and all eat plants. The males are known for the musical sounds they make by rubbing together the roughened edges of their wings or legs.

Isopods—Pill Bugs and Sow Bugs

The name isopod ("same foot" in Latin) describes how these crustaceans have legs and feet that look the same. The pill bug does, as its name suggests, roll into a ball when disturbed. Sow bugs are flatter, faster, can't roll up, and have a pair of sensors that stick out at their back end. *Count the pairs of legs.*

Lacewings

Green and brown lacewings are common throughout the woods and fields of North America. The larvae of these beautiful net-winged insects are predators. Green lacewings are raised commercially and released in vineyards and greenhouses to control mealybugs.

Leafhoppers

The acrobatic leafhoppers and treehoppers will move sideways, hop, and fly. Some are bright green, others look like thorns, and many are colored with bright patterns. The size of rice grains, these insects are very numerous during the warm months, sucking plant juices for food. *Release some leafhoppers into a large box to observe how many times their body length these circus stars can jump.*

Millipedes

These worm-like, armored animals are harmless and very slow moving. Sometimes they coil into a spiral for protection. They are crustaceans, and are beneficial scavengers, helping to recycle Nature's waste. *How do you think millipedes got their name?*

Mites

These very tiny spider-like animals have eight legs. They look like fast moving dots. Colors vary; red, orange, brown, and black are most common. Some mites are predators, eating the eggs of small animals like aphids and roundworms; others feed on plants and decaying vegetation.

Snails and Slugs

Most of their relatives live in the ocean or in lakes and streams. Land snails and slugs secrete a slippery substance on which they travel, leaving a silvery track to mark their passage. They eat fresh and decaying plant material.

Spiders

These amazing predators are found almost everywhere—on the ground, among grasses, hiding in tree branches, and in the crevices of buildings and fences. Some spiders pounce on their prey, while others build webs, but all make silken sacs to protect their eggs.

Ticks

Ticks have eight legs and two body regions like their distant relatives, the spiders. They are ectoparasites and feed on the blood of reptiles, birds, and mammals. The nymphs of some ticks are smaller than the head of a pin, and the even smaller larvae have six legs. Adult ticks can be the size of a small raisin. Ticks can transmit dangerous diseases to humans. **If you find a tick, don't touch it, and have your teacher save it for identification.**

Spider Web Identification Key

Warning! Almost all spiders have some kind of poison. It's often only enough to give you a small bump, but sometimes can be dangerous. For this reason it is best not to handle spiders.

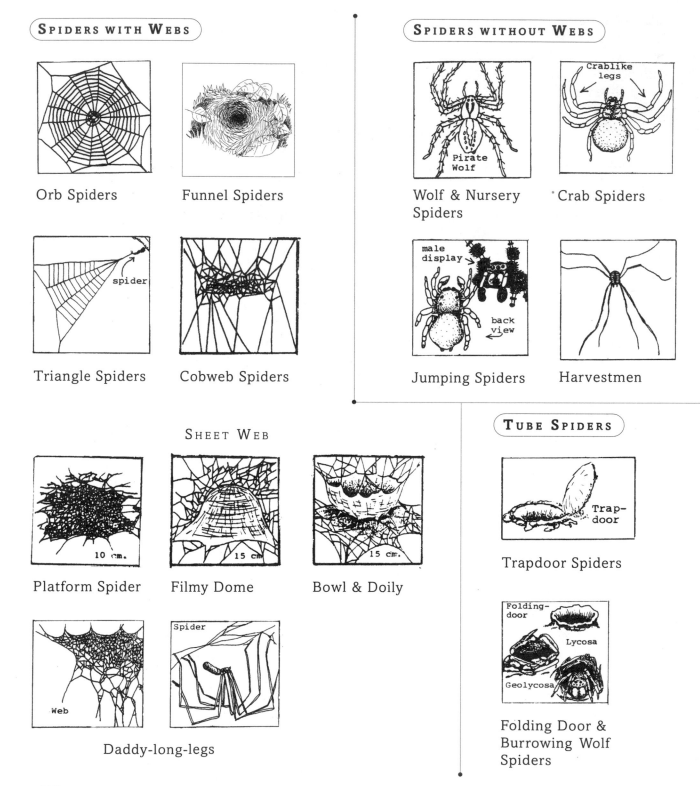

SPIDERS WITH WEBS

Orb Spiders

Funnel Spiders

Triangle Spiders

Cobweb Spiders

SHEET WEB

Platform Spider

Filmy Dome

Bowl & Doily

Daddy-long-legs

SPIDERS WITHOUT WEBS

Pirate Wolf

Wolf & Nursery Spiders

Crablike legs

Crab Spiders

male display

back view

Jumping Spiders

Harvestmen

TUBE SPIDERS

Trapdoor

Trapdoor Spiders

Folding-door

Lycosa

Geolycosa

Folding Door & Burrowing Wolf Spiders

SPIDERS WITH WEBS

- **Orb Web Weavers** *(Argiopidae or Araneidae)*—This is the round "Charlotte's Web," a work of art and engineering.

Fun Facts—Orb spiders live alone, and usually eat other spiders they meet. The motto of the female orb spider might be that "a husband's place is in the stomach of his wife." In other words, a female orb spider would eat her former mate just as she would any other hunk of meat, such as an insect.

Their Webs—Most orb spiders eat and then rebuild at least part of their web every day or night. Their webs are almost like another part of their bodies. They use them to catch meals and to sense the world around them. Orb spiders have very poor eyesight, but they don't need to see well, because they use their webs to **feel** the world around them. They have special lines in their webs that are like doorbells, because when something touches them, they vibrate, and the vibrations are a message to the spider. The spider can tell by the way the web vibrates if the movements are from a male spider looking for a mate, a delicious struggling insect victim, or something else. If these lines were cut, the spider's main sense would be cut off, and it would not be able to sense any movement in its web.

Preparing the trap—The spider squirts sticky drops on its web and then "twangs" the web (like a string on a bow) with its leg. This spreads the sticky drops along the silk lines. When they catch an insect, orb spiders use their front legs to quickly spin their captive. At the same time, they use their back legs to pull out silk and wrap the victim like a mummy.

- **Triangle Web Weavers** *(Uloboridae Hyptiotes)*—Look for the spider that builds this triangle-shaped "piece of pie" web where the thread attaches to the branch.

Fun Facts—The spider waits, its body stretched out, holding the web tight. When an insect flies into the trap, the spider shakes the line several times, which makes the insect more and more tangled up in the web. With the insect helplessly stuck, the spider can walk down to it for a meal. This is one of the very few spiders which does not have poison in its fangs.

- **Funnel Web Weavers** *(Agelenidae)*—Most Funnel web spiders spin platform webs leading to a silk tube.

Fun Facts—Imagine running through deep snow while being chased by someone on skis. That's how helpless an insect victim of this spider might feel. This spider's silk is not sticky, and insects land on the web and find it hard to move around on its funnel shape and may bounce, like on a trampoline. The funnel web spiders can run quickly on top of the

inside the drawings

├──────┤ = actual spider body length

Orb Spiders

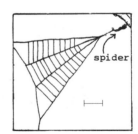

Triangle Spiders

Funnel Spiders

web, grab their struggling victims, and return with them to their funnel to eat them. The back end of their funnel is open, so it can be used to escape when threatened. The males often move in and share the female's web after mating. In fall, the females hide their eggs under bark or leaves, not in their web.

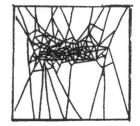

Cobweb Spiders

- **Cobweb Weavers or Comb-footed spiders** *(Theriidae)*—The webs made by spiders in this family are irregular, usually with a platform with threads going up and down above and below it. The threads are sticky and tough, and the webs can be found in cracks, and underneath leaves, rocks or loose bark. This large family has many kinds of spiders in it, including the poisonous black widow. Be very careful not to touch these spiders, and do not reach under rocks or logs without looking.

Fun Facts—Cobweb spiders set "booby traps" to catch insects that crawl on the ground. They put sticky drops at the ends of silk lines where they connect to the ground. An insect may walk by, get caught in one of these sticky drops and try to get away. The silk line then breaks off of the ground like a rubber band, snapping the victim into the center of the web—and to its doom. As it struggles, it gets tangled up in other threads. These spiders are called comb-footed because they have tiny combs of hairs on their back pair of legs. They use these to comb silk out of their spinnerets to wrap their prey.

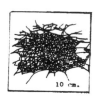

Platform Spider   Filmy Dome

Bowl & Doily

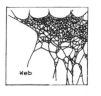

Daddy-long-legs

Sheet Web Weavers *(Linyphiidae)*

- **Platform Spider** *(Microlinyphia sp.)*
- **Filmy Dome Spiders** *(Linyphia marginata)*
- **Bowl and Doily Spiders** *(Frontinella pyramitela)*
  These spiders usually hang upside down underneath their platform, dome, or bowl—waiting for prey.

Fun Facts—Their webs have "booby trap" trip threads that break when flying insects crash into them. The threads snap like rubber bands, knocking the insect into the silk web to their doom. The spider grabs the victim through the web and pulls it underneath, where it is eaten. Because the insects rip their webs, they have to fix their webs after every catch. The males and females often live together in the same web.

- **Daddy-long-legs Spiders** *(Pholcidae)*—You'll find these spiders hanging upside down in loose, irregular "mish-mash" webs in corners of houses or cellars.

Fun Facts—These are the "true" Daddy-long-legs, often confused with Harvestmen (see below). These spiders have long, thin legs. If you scare them, some shake their webs to try to make themselves and their web blur and seem to disappear. The female carries her round egg sac in her jaws like a dog carries a ball.

SPIDERS WITHOUT WEBS

- **Wolf Spiders** *(Lycosidae)*—These are among the most common spiders.

Fun Facts—Instead of making webs, these spiders chase down their prey, like lone wolves. They run around on the ground and some climb plants, leaving a silk "drag line" wherever they go. Some hunt during the day and some at night, and they rest under stones or wood in silk "sleeping bags." The male finds a female to mate with by following her dragline. To convince her that he's a date and not a meal, he waves his pedipalps in a pattern as he approaches her. After mating, her mood changes, and she may try to eat him. After the eggs are laid, the female carries her large egg sac around like a tiny basketball attached to her rear end. When the young hatch, they hang on to their mom's abdomen for weeks or months, but after they leave, she may eat them. Some Pirate Wolf spiders, which can be identified by a black V-shaped mark on their backs (see picture) can run on top of water.

Wolf & Nursery Spiders

- **Nursery Web Spiders** *(Pisauridae)*—These look a lot like Wolf spiders. They can be told apart from Pirate Wolf Spiders because they don't have a dark V-shape (see above).

Fun Facts—Many can run on the surface of water and even dive and stay underwater for some time. The females tie leaves together with silk and put their egg sac inside. They protect the egg sac until the young hatch.

- **Jumping Spiders** *(Salticidae)*—Like some energetic people, these spiders are usually brightly colored, active during the day, and love sunshine. They walk irregularly, with a lot of stops and starts, and jump on their prey. They are easy to tell apart from other spiders, because they have four big eyes on the face, and four smaller ones on top of the head.

Jumping Spiders

Fun Facts—Jumping spiders sometimes jump 40 times their own length. Try multiplying your height by 40 and see how far you would have to jump to do this. Before jumping, the spider attaches a silk thread so it can climb back in case it goofs and misses. Because they use their eyes to find prey, jumping spiders have the best eyes of any spiders, and among the best of all animals without backbones.

Dating—People often dance on dates, and so do jumping spiders. After finding a female by following her silk dragline, the male does a courtship dance. He waves his brightly colored first legs in front of the female, wags his abdomen, and hops. If the female is of the same species, she signals with her legs, to "Come on over."

- **Crab Spiders** *(Thomisidae)*

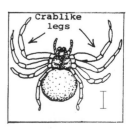
Crab Spiders

Fun Facts—These spiders hold their legs out at the sides like crabs and can walk forward, backwards, or sideways. Crab spiders wait in ambush for passing insects. Some are brightly colored and wait inside flowers to ambush bees and other insects.

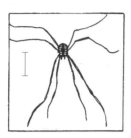

Harvestmen

• **Harvestmen** *(Phalangiidae, order Opiliones, suborder Palapatroes)*

AHA !! Caught you! These are spider "cousins," *not* real spiders. Spiders have bodies clearly divided into two parts, abdomen and cephalothorax. Although Harvestmen also have these two parts, they *appear* not to—in other words—they don't have a "waistline." They are called Harvestmen because when first scientifically described, they were seen at harvest time.

Fun Facts—Harvestmen clean their long, thin legs by pulling them between their jaws. They can't make silk and they eat very small insects. Since real spiders often eat each other, for them mating can be dangerous. That is not the case with Harvestmen, who eat tiny insects. They can easily mate with any number of partners of the opposite sex they meet.

TUBE SPIDERS

Trapdoor Spiders

• **Trapdoor spiders** *(Ctenizidae)*—These tarantulas dig tube-like burrows that are lined with silk. The top of the lid may be hard to find, because it is camouflaged with leaves, twigs or whatever may be lying around.

Fun Facts—The lid may be held shut by the spider, sometimes with an amazing amount of force. The trap-door spider makes many silk "telegraph lines" around its burrow, then waits inside for a vibration that tells it that an insect is walking by. It then rushes out, grabs the prey, and pulls it into the tube where it is eaten.

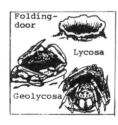

Folding Door & Burrowing Wolf Spiders

• **Folding Door Spiders** *(Antrodiaetidae)*—Folding door spiders are also tarantulas. They do not close the opening of their tubes with a trap door. Instead, some close their tubes by pulling in the rim.

• **Burrowing Wolf Spiders** *(Lycosa and Geolycosa)*

Fun Facts—Some Burrowing spiders dig shallow holes under rocks. Others use their strong front legs to dig tubes into the ground up to 12 inches deep. Some wrap sand with silk as they dig, and toss the little "packages" out around their holes. The sand from different colored layers of dirt may make rings around the burrow. These spiders spend almost their whole lives in the doorway of their burrows, waiting for some action. They can feel ground vibrations very well, and run underground at any sign of danger. When it's sunny, females sometimes bring their egg sacs up to dry like laundry.

Resources

Related Curriculum Material

There are a wealth of curriculum materials relating to ecology and the environment. To explore the many units available, we recommend that you check out resources such as the National Science Resources Center publication entitled *Resources for Teaching Elementary School Science*, National Academy Press, Washington, D.C. 1996, and *NSTA Pathways to the Science Standards*, Lawrence F. Lowery, editor, National Science Teachers Association, Arlington, Virginia, 1997. Both books include listings and annotations of life science, ecology, and environmental units that would nicely complement or extend the activities in *Schoolyard Ecology*. You will also find many curriculum materials recommended in publications of leading environmental education organizations and others highlighted on the internet, as well as many related units on insects and plants. We welcome your suggestions.

This GEMS teacher's guide owes an important part of its inspiration to the multiplicity of activities found in the **Outdoor Biology Instructional Strategies (OBIS)** program, developed at the Lawrence Hall of Science and available from Delta Education (1-800-258-1302). OBIS modules such as Outdoor Study Techniques, Child's Play, Schoolyard, Backyard, Bio-Crafts, Adaptations, Animal Behavior, Lawns and Fields, Outdoor Study Techniques, and many others bring together an innovative and highly effective series of activities in many natural settings.

The **Full Option Science System (FOSS),** developed at the Lawrence Hall of Science, includes a number of excellent modules that relate to the activities in this GEMS guide. FOSS modules for Grades 1 and 2 include **New Plants** and **Insects.** In the **New Plants** module (4 activities) students become familiar with the structures of flowering plants and discover ways to propagate new plants from mature plants. Students grow plants from seed, as well as from cuttings, bulbs, and roots, and monitor growth. The **Insects** module (6 activities) introduces students to the life cycles of many insects, including darkling beetles, milkweed bugs, wax and silk moths, painted lady butterflies, crickets, and ants. For Grades 3 and 4, the FOSS **Structures of Life** module (5 activities) features seeds germination in hydroponic gardens and classroom observation of crayfish. The **Environments** module, for Grades 5 and 6 (6 activities) provides structured investigations in both terrestrial and aquatic systems to develop concepts of environmental factor, tolerance, environmental preference, and environmental range. FOSS modules are available from Delta Education, 5 Hudson Park Drive, Hudson, New Hampshire 03051-0915, (800) 258-1302.

The **Science Activities for the Visually Impaired/Science Enrichment for Learners with Physical Handicaps (SAVI/SELPH)** program, from the Lawrence Hall of Science, includes an Environments module for Grades 4–7 with four activities in which students investigate the concept of environment and learn what factors in an organism's environment make it an appropriate place in which to live. Experiments test for water requirements and salt tolerance in plants, and for environmental preferences of isopods. A culminating activity takes children to the schoolyard for close observation of local weeds, their structure and habitat. Available from the Center for Multisensory Learning, 510-642-8941.

The **Science Curriculum Improvement Study 3 (SCIS3)**, originally developed at the Lawrence Hall of Science (available from Delta Education, 1-800-258-1302) includes, for Grades 5 and 6, an Ecosystems unit in which students study the factors that make up an ecosystem, a Populations unit where students explore the interrelationships of organisms and their populations, a Life Cycles unit, and an Environments unit with terrariums. In addition, the SCIS3 Communities unit emphasizes the interdependent populations in any given area. Students dissect and identify parts of a seed, plant seeds in a terrarium, and learn about food chains. They add animals to the terrarium and discover plant eaters, animal eaters, and decomposers.

The **Life Lab Science Program** (available from Videodiscovery, 1-800-548-3472) includes, for Grades 3 and 4, a Structure-Function unit, in which students use their gardens to study the structures of plants and animals in a habitat, and a Connections unit, where students study interactions in and around their gardens, exploring concepts such as food webs, nutrient conservation, and ecosystems.

Science and Technology for Children (STC) from the National Science Resources Center, the Smithsonian Institution, and National Academy of Sciences (available from Carolina Biological Supply Company, 1-800-334-5551) includes a Plant Growth and Development unit for Grades 3–4 and, for Grades 5–6, an Experiments with Plants unit and an Ecosystems unit, in which students study the interdependence of living and non-living elements in their environment and maintain a terrarium and an aquarium.

The Science for Life and Living (BSCS) curriculum from The Biological Science Curriculum Study (available from Kendall/Hunt Publishing, 1-800-542-6657) includes a unit for Grades 5 and 6 on Ecosystems and Resources. In this unit, students make decisions about how to manage ecosystems for the benefit of plants and animals.

The Missouri Botanical Garden (Suitcase Science) in St. Louis, Missouri (314-577-5149) produces a number of environmentally-related programs, including Urban Gardening, for Grades K–9. Students are encouraged to consider the city environment, to plan and plant a garden, and to study the small ecosystems they have created.

Institute of Ecosystem Studies
Box AB
Millbrook, NY 12545
(914) 677-5343
http://vm.marist.edu:80/~ies/

This independent not-for-profit corporation, founded in 1983, is one of the largest centers of ecological research in North America. To quote from the institute's own Mission Statement, the institute "is dedicated to the creation, dissemination, and application of knowledge about ecological systems. This knowledge is created through scientific research, disseminated through teaching, writing, and exhibits, and applied through participation in decision-making regarding the ecological management of natural resources and through promotion of a broader awareness about the importance of ecological relationships to human welfare."

Two special public-education programs they offer are SYEFEST (Schoolyard Ecology for Elementary School Teachers) and EcoInquiry (a middle school curriculum in ecology). They have a free newsletter entitled *Schoolyard Ecology News* and are currently working on a publication entitled *Schoolyard Ecology Leader's Handbook* which contains activities that help teachers learn how to do ecologically-related activities with students.

Acorn Naturalists Catalog
17300 East 17th Street, #J-236
Tustin, CA 92780
(800) 422-8886
http://www.acorn-group.com

This catalog is filled with resources for exploring the natural world. It contains a myriad of materials such as field guides, equipment, puppets, and a large variety of books—including several on understanding and developing environmental education programs.

General Resources

Books

Backyard Insects, Millicent Ellis Selsam, Four Winds Press, New York, 1981.
> Text and photographs discuss common garden insects and their protective appearance which includes camouflage, warning colors, copycat characteristics, and scary characteristics.

Bug Wise: Thirty Incredible Insect Investigations and Arachnid Activities, Pamela M. Hickman, Addison-Wesley Publishing, Reading, Massachusetts, 1990.
> Text, illustrations, questions and answers, and suggested activities introduce the world of insects and other arthropods.

Bugs, Nancy Winslow Parker and Joan Richards Wright, Greenwillow Books, New York, 1987.
> Includes general information, jokes, and brief descriptions of the physical characteristics, habits, and natural environment of a variety of common insects.

Bugs for Dinner? The Eating Habits of Neighborhood Creatures, Sam and Beryl Epstein, Macmillan Publishing, New York, 1989.
> Recounts how squirrels, grasshoppers, ants, spiders, and other creatures in an urban environment find their food and avoid being eaten themselves.

The City Kid's Field Guide, Ethan Herberman, Simon & Schuster Books for Young Readers, New York, 1989.
> Describes the wildlife commonly found in a variety of urban environments, including backyards, vacant lots, parks, and city margins.

Cricketology; Rolypolyology; Snailology; Wormology, Michael Elsohn Ross, Carolrhoda Books, Minneapolis, 1996.
> Developed to encourage individual study and observation skills, this "Backyard Buddies Series" introduces young readers to the biology, life cycle, and habits of several common creatures. Each title includes tips on

where to find the creatures and instructions for a wide variety of simple activities and science experiments readers can conduct in order to answer their own questions about the subject.

The Golden Book of Insects and Spiders, Laurence Pringle, Western Publishing Company, Racine, Wisconsin, 1990.
An examination of a variety of insects and spiders and their unique behaviors.

Insects & Spiders, Penny Clarke, Franklin Watts, New York, 1995.
Describes the physical characteristics, lifestyles, and environmental effects of such insects as ants, beetles, flies, and spiders.

Insects: How to Watch and Understand the Busy World of Insects, Steve Parker, Dorling Kindersley, New York, 1992.
Describes the physical characteristics, behavior, and metamorphosis of insects and examines kinds of garden insects, woodland insects, and others.

Nature in Your Backyard: Simple Activities for Children, Susan S. Lang with the staff of Cayuga Nature Center, Millbrook Press, Brookfield, Connecticut, 1995.
Through a series of projects, experiments, and activities, this book presents the natural world that's right outside the door.

Nature's Great Balancing Act: In Our Own Backyard, E. Jaediker Norsgaard, Dutton, New York, 1990.
Discusses the interrelationship of all the creatures and plants in nature, emphasizing the importance of insects.

One Small Square: Backyard, Donald M. Silver, W. H. Freeman, New York, 1993.
Explains how to observe and explore plants, animals, and their interactions in your own backyard.

Pet Bugs: A Kid's Guide to Catching and Keeping Touchable Insects, Sally Kneidel, Wiley, New York, 1994.
> Descriptions and interesting information about the behavior of many insects and insect relatives as well as information on where to find them and how to catch and keep them in captivity.

Who Eats What? Food Chains and Food Webs, Patricia Lauber, HarperCollins, New York, 1995.
> Explains the concept of a food chain and how plants, animals, and humans are ecologically linked. Every link in the food chain is important because each living thing depends on others for survival.

Wings, Stings and Wriggly Things, Martin Jenkins, Candlewick Press, Cambridge, Massachusetts, 1996.
> Offers a close-up look at animals such as butterflies, snails, bees, dragonflies, spiders, and more through easy-to-read text, large illustrations, picture strips, and foldout pages.

The World of Insects, Susanne Santoro Whayne, Simon & Schuster Books for Young Readers, New York, 1990.
> Describes the life cycles, physical characteristics, and behavior of a variety of insects.

Field Guides

A Field Guide to the Insects of America North of Mexico, Donald Borror and Richard White, Houghton Mifflin, Boston, 1970.

A Golden Guide: Ecology, Taylor R. Alexander and George S. Fichter, Western Publishing Company, New York, 1973.

Insects: A Guide to Familiar American Insects, Herbert S. Zim and Clarence Cottam, Golden Press, New York, 1961.

The National Audubon Society Field Guide to North American Insects & Spiders, Lorus and Margery Milne, Alfred A. Knopf, New York, 1980.

Peterson First Guide to Insects of North America, Christopher Leahy, Houghton Mifflin, Boston, 1987.

Simon & Schuster Children's Guide to Insects and Spiders, Jinny Johnson, Simon & Schuster Books for Young People, New York, 1997.

Video

Insects and Spiders Up Close, Warren A. Hatch Productions, 1996.
> This 37 minute video shows extreme close ups made possible by a video microscope. You may want to show just selections of the video to your students as the quality of the footage varies. Order directly from Warren Hatch, P.O. Box 9224, Portland, OR 97207. Hatch has many other videos, including one to accompany the GEMS guide *Microscopic Explorations.*

Mapping

Maps & Mazes: A First Guide to Mapmaking, Gillian Chapman and Pam Robson, Millbrook Press, Brookfield, Connecticut, 1993.

Spider Resources

Books

Amazing Spiders, Alexandra Parsons, Alfred A. Knopf, New York, 1990.
> Text and photographs introduce some of the most amazing members of the spider family, such as fish-eating spiders, spitting spiders, and banana spiders.

Amazing Spiders, Claudia Schnieper, Carolrhoda Books, Minneapolis, 1989.
> Introduces the varieties, appearance, behavior, and life cycles of spiders.

The Book of Spiders and Scorpions, Rod Preston-Mafham, Crescent Books, New York, 1991.

Extremely Weird Spiders, Sarah Lovett, John Muir Publications, Santa Fe, New Mexico, 1991.

The Fascinating World of Spiders, Maria Angels Julivert, Barron's, Hauppauge, New York, 1992.
> An introduction to the physical characteristics, habits, and natural environment of various kinds of spiders.

Spider Watching, Vivian French, Candlewick Press, Cambridge, Massachusetts, 1994.

Spiders, Zoobooks, Wildlife Education Ltd., San Diego, 1992.

Spider's Nest, Kate Scarborough, Time-Life Books, New York, 1997.
> Follows the step-by-step process of a female trap-door spider building her nest, catching prey, and laying eggs.

Spider's Web, Christine Back, Silver Burdett, Morristown, New Jersey, 1986.
> Text and photographs describe how a garden spider spins her web and how she uses it to catch food.

Spotlight on Spiders, Densey Clyne, Allen & Unwin, St. Leonards, NSW, Australia, 1995.
> Focuses on the hunting techniques, mating behaviors, and egg laying of a variety of exotic spiders.

Web Weavers and Other Spiders, Bobbie Kalman, Crabtree Publishing, New York, 1997.
> This book provides an overview of spiders, covering their physical characteristics, web-building, mating behavior, and defense techniques.

Magazine articles

"Portia Spider: Mistress of Deception," Robert R. Jackson, *National Geographic,* Vol. 190, No. 5, November 1996, pages 104–115.

"Spider Spit and Other Bits," Deborah Churchman, *Ranger Rick,* Vol. 30, No. 11, November 1996, pages 26–27.

"Super Spider Silk," Deborah Churchman, *Ranger Rick,* Vol. 29, No. 5, May 1995, pages 36–43.

Video

Like Jake and Me, Disney Educational Productions, Walt Disney Educational Media, Northbrook, Illinois; distributed by Coronet/MTI Film & Video, 1989.
> A 13 minute and 50 seconds-long videorecording based on a book with the same title. See the "Literature Connections" section, page 99.

Web sites (great pun, isn't it?—spider *web* sites)

Arachnology
> http://dns.ufsia.ac.be/Arachnology/Arachnology.html

Arachnology for the Young Ones
> http://dns.ufsia.ac.be/Arachnology/Pages/Kids.html

Arachnida
> http://www.york.biosis.org/zrdocs/zoolinfo/grp_arac.htm

Tim Tesseret's Page of Spiders
> http://www.mtco.com/~brent/spider.htm

Spiders of Europe
> http://www.xs4all.nl/~ednieuw/index.html

Australian spiders
> http://www.xs4all.nl/~ednieuw/australian/Spidaus.html

Ant Resources

Books

A Look at Ants, Ross E. Hutchins, Dodd, Mead and Company, New York, 1978.
> Describes the physical characteristics, habits, and natural environment of various kinds of ants.

All Upon A Sidewalk, Jean Craighead George, Dutton, New York, 1974.
> Relates the experiences of a city-dwelling ant as she seeks sugar for the ant community.

An Ant Colony, Heiderose and Andreas Fischer-Nagel, Carolrhoda Books, Minneapolis, 1989.
> Describes the life cycle and community life of ants.

Ant Cities, Arthur Dorros, Thomas Y. Crowell, New York, 1987.
> Explains how ants live and work together to build and maintain their cities.

Ants, Cynthia Overbeck, Lerner Publications, Minneapolis, 1982.
> Describes the characteristics and behavior of ants that build nests for storing food and raising their young, ants that spend most of their time traveling, and ants that invade the nests of other ants.

Armies of Ants, Walter Retan, Scholastic, New York, 1994.

Discovering Ants, Christopher O'Toole, The Bookwright Press, New York, 1986.

The Fascinating World of Ants, Maria Angels Julivert, Barron's, Hauppauge, New York, 1991.

The Life Cycle of an Ant, Trevor Terry and Margaret Linton, The Bookwright Press, New York, 1988.

Looking At Ants, Dorothy Hinshaw Patent, Holiday House, New York, 1989.
> Examines the physical characteristics, behavior, methods of communication, and ecological significance of ants.

questions and answers about Ants, Millicent E. Selsam, Four
Winds Press, New York, 1967.

> Answers questions such as: What do ants eat? How do
> ants find their way? Can ants learn? Explains the
> habits and behavior of ordinary ants and tells how to
> keep ants.

Thinking About Ants, Barbara Brenner, Mondo Publishing,
Greenvale, New York, 1997.

> Asks the reader to imagine what it would be like to be
> an ant, describing what ants look like, what they eat,
> where and how they live, and more.

Computer Software

"SimAnt," Maxis Software, 2121 N. California Blvd., Suite
600, Walnut Creek, CA 94596-3572   (800) 336-2947.

> SimAnt is a simulation/learning game like the well
> known SimCity or SimEarth. In SimAnt, a player is to
> imagine they're the leader of a colony of black ants
> living in a back yard whose mission is to fight off an
> invasion of red ants and human influences, then take
> over the yard and house. On two separate graphs, the
> player can set the number of workers, breeders, and
> soldiers in the colony and control the percent of forag-
> ers, diggers, and nurses. There are maps of under-
> ground and above ground habitats and grid-like
> representations of the yard and house. In addition to
> the simulation, there is a lab feature. In this experimen-
> tal mode, a player can place all kinds of objects to see
> how the simAnts react.

> SimAnt has quite a bit to do with ants, and students
> could learn quite a bit from it. Maxis Software recom-
> mends it for ages 8 and up. To evaluate whether the
> software is appropriate for their students, interested
> teachers could visit the Maxis home page at http://
> www.maxis.com/index.html and go to the Sim Ant site
> where the game is explained and several screens are
> shown. For classrooms the game could be rented,
> rather than purchased, from a local video store to
> lessen the investment.

Music Resources

"Rocking the Foundations of Science"(1994) and "Rock Candy"(1997), Bungee Jumpin' Cows, C.U.D. Productions, 413A 61st Street, Oakland, CA 94609, (888) 434-COWS, www.moo-boing.com/bjc

> Developed and performed by a group of science-teacher musicians, this tape contains many creative songs. For *Schoolyard Ecology,* the most appropriate song is "Arachnidae"—a funk tune about spiders' eating, web making, and mating behaviors. Please see the next page for the music and lyrics to "Arachnidae."

"Adventures on the Air Cycle," Banana Slug String Band, Music for Little People, Redway, California, 1989.

> Piloting his wondrous "Fresh Air Cycle," the Nature Man transports inquisitive children to the world's habitats and shows how everything fits together naturally. Songs relevant to *Schoolyard Ecology* include "Everything Needs A Home," "Ecology," and "No Bones Within"—a song about insects with a catchy chorus: head, thorax, abdomen; we're inside-out, no bones within.

"Penguin Parade," Banana Slug String Band, Music for Little People, Redway, California, 1996.

> Contains many fun and educational songs, including one entitled "What Do Animals Need?"—a rap-style song about habitat and the environmental needs of animals.

Arachnidae

By Pete Madsen, Kevin Beals & Mel McMurrin

I think I hear the doorbell   I   guess it's time to eat   My

web   it   is a-jigglin'   from some   insect's   tiny feet   I'll

wrap you   up in   silk then   I'll   eat your insides   raw   You'll

be my insect   smoothie, suck your   guts like with a straw   It's

killer tag   and   I'm it,   don't you want to play   (NO WAY!)

I just   want to wish you an   arachnid   DAY

Webs can be triangular, funnel-shaped, or round
Some have sticky trip lines, some dig down in the ground
Others they don't have webs they chase down their prey
I'm so glad to meet you but I guess it's not your day

When it's time to mate, it's a dangerous dating game
Some spiders eat each other, things that wiggle are all the same
The females have a motto that means I risk my life—
A husband's place is inside the stomach of his wife

93

Assessment Suggestions

Selected Student Outcomes

1. Students can identify several environmental factors—such as sunlight, cover, and moisture—that can be used to distinguish differing environments and which may influence the abundance of animals in an area.

2. Students improve their ability to make careful observations of environmental characteristics and animal physical features/behaviors, using basic investigative techniques and recording their observations in journals.

3. Students are able to accurately record information on animals and environmental characteristics on maps of the schoolyard, and analyze a map to learn more about the relationship of animal communities to the physical environment.

4. Students develop responsible behaviors toward and appreciation for animals, plants, and the environment.

Built-in Assessment Activities

The Schoolyard. In Activity 1: Exploring the Schoolyard Study Area pairs of students use their senses to observe environmental characteristics of the schoolyard. Later, students map the area, recording areas of high and low moisture, sunlight, and cover. As the students are working, the teacher can circulate among the teams asking for their reasoning in selecting the areas of extremes for each factor, as well as observing if they are accurately recording the locations on the map. Journal entries can be reviewed for detailed and accurate observations. (Outcomes 1, 2, 3)

Animal Communities. In Activities 2 through 4, students have the opportunity to investigate and map the presence of spiders, ants, and other plant-dwelling animals in the schoolyard environment. They make detailed drawings of the animals on cards and sort the cards to compare similarities and differences. During class discussions and map-analysis sessions, the teacher can observe if students are able to identify and discuss the relationship between animals and the physical environment. The teacher can review journal entries and drawings, and have students share their observations with the class, to evaluate their understanding of animal diversity and appreciation for the environment and living things. (Outcomes 1, 2, 3, 4)

Study Sites. In Activity 5: Special Study Sites, students define a small study area with a string loop and mark the location on a map. Using knowledge and observation strategies gained from the previous activities, students investigate, map, and analyze the plants, animals, and environmental factors of their study site. The teacher can ask students to explain the relationship of the animal communities to the physical site in their journal or during a class discussion and assess how students are applying previous knowledge to a new situation. (Outcomes 1, 2, 3, 4)

Additional Assessment Ideas

What Do You Know? (Pre- and Post-). Prior to the series of activities in the unit, ask students to make a list, which can include drawings, of the things they know about spiders and ants. Collect the lists and save them for later. At the end of the unit, hand back their papers for students to review. Have them use another color of ink or pencil to add any new things they have learned. They may want to correct misconceptions on the original list. Provide time for students to share their advances in knowledge! (Outcome 2)

Adventure Stories. Students can go out to observe a spider or an insect, then write adventure stories, as described in the "Going Further" suggestion for Activity 2, and exemplified in the optional reading "Tales from the Web." Explain to students that their adventure stories must be realistic and include at least 10 direct observations. Stories can be evaluated based on student ability to make and communicate detailed observations, and to bring together facts and observations in a creative manner. (Outcomes 1, 2, 4)

What If? Have students imagine they are an animal or plant living in their study site. Encourage them to write about what they would experience in the site as the school year goes by. (Outcomes 1, 2, 4)

Study Sites Continued. Encourage students to observe the changes that take place in their study site over the next few months and record those changes on maps and in journals. Have them include predictions, and as changes take place, make inferences about why those changes occurred. (Outcomes 1, 2, 3, 4)

More Animals. Find another prevalent animal in your schoolyard to observe such as birds. Investigate the bird population, mapping their locations, and observing their relationship to the other plants, animals, and physical factors of the schoolyard. (Outcomes 1, 2, 3, 4)

Environmental Authors. Encourage students to write an essay in the environmental writing tradition of Thoreau, Muir, or the many modern writers who have made careful observation of the environment a hallmark of their craft. Students could write about their study site or could select a well-known environmental feature in the region to visit and describe. (Outcomes 2, 4)

For more on GEMS and assessment, consult *Insights & Outcomes: Assessments for Great Explorations in Math and Science* (also known as the "GEMS assessment handbook"). The handbook includes 17 case studies from the GEMS series, with student work, to illustrate different modes of assessment and show how student work can be evaluated. One case study, a writing activity drawn from the GEMS guide *Terrarium Habitats* which asks students to describe their life as an isopod, parallels possible writing assignments in *Schoolyard Ecology*. The handbook also examines the GEMS approach to assessment through the lens of two teachers presenting GEMS curriculum sequences over the course of the school year and includes a compendium of selected student outcomes, built-in assessments, and additional assessment ideas for guides in the GEMS series. Contact the GEMS National Office for more information.

Literature Connections

Anansi the Spider: A Tale from the Ashanti
by Gerald McDermott
Holt, Rinehart and Winston, New York. 1972
Grades: K–4

Anansi, a folk hero to the Ashanti people of Ghana, Africa, is a wise and loveable trickster. In this story he wanders far from home, gets lost, and falls into trouble. His six sons all play a part in his rescue and Anansi is unsure which one to reward. Because of his inability to decide, Anansi is responsible for placing the moon in the sky.

Antics!
by Cathi Hepworth
G. P. Putnam's Sons, New York. 1992
Grades: All ages

For a totally humorous and very humanized view of ants, this is a great book. It is an alphabetical **ant**hology of funny "ant" words. Each page has a large, richly detailed illustration of the word. For example, "A" is for **Ant**ique and the illustration shows a very old ant sitting in a rocker on a porch while knitting and listening to a gramophone. Many pages contain several funnies—the initial pun with the "ant" word plus more in the illustration.

Charlotte's Web
by E.B. White; illustrated by Garth Williams
Harper & Row, New York. 1952
Grades: 4–7

This classic story tells of the friendship between a wise gray spider named Charlotte and a pig named Wilbur. Although most of the story centers around the anthropomorphised animals, Charlotte offers many cogent observations on web spinning and egg sacs, the natural cycle of life-death-reproduction, and the lasting value of friendship.

City Green
by DyAnne DiSalvo-Ryan
Morrow Junior Books, New York. 1994
Grades: K–5

While planting some flowers, Marcy, an African American girl, and her good friend Miss Rosa have an idea to plant more in the vacant lot next to their apartment building. They gather signatures on a petition showing neighborhood interest in the project and obtain a lease from the city. Many neighbors pitch in to help and soon the lot is transformed into a community garden filled with flowers and vegetables.

The City Under the Back Steps
by Evelyn Sibley Lampman; illustrated by Honoré Valintcourt
Doubleday, Garden City, New York. 1960
Grades: 4–7

While Craig and his cousin Jill are sitting on the back steps watching ants scurry into a hole, something magical happens and they shrink down to ant size and are escorted into the ants' chambers. They become pets of the queen and help out in the ant colony. Through the story, the reader learns quite a bit about ants and their society.

The Earth is Painted Green: A Garden of Poems About Our Planet
edited by Barbara Brenner; illustrated by S.D. Schindler
Scholastic, New York. 1994
Grades: All ages

The poems of such notable authors as Margaret Wise Brown, Myra Cohn Livingston, Carl Sandburg, and Shel Silverstein are assembled into this collection which celebrates our green planet. Rich watercolor illustrations complete the image the poems conjure.

The Empty Lot
by Dale H. Fife; illustrated by Jim Arnosky
Sierra Club Books/Little, Brown, Boston. 1991
Grades: 2–4

What good is a vacant lot? City-dweller Harry Hale owns one, and when he looks it over before selling it, he is amazed to find that the lot is far from empty. It's pulsing with life: birds and their nests; ants, beetles, fungi, and molds in the soil; and frogs and dragonflies near the stream. A nice connection to the often hidden life students are likely to find in the schoolyard.

Fly Away, Fly Away Over the Sea: and Other Poems for Children
by Christina Rossetti; selected and illustrated by Bernadette Watts
North-South Books, New York. 1991
Grades: All ages

A collection of classic poems including "Hurt No Living Thing" which features many different insects. The poems provide a nice example of writing inspired by observations of the natural world.

Grandmother Spider Brings the Sun: A Cherokee Story
by Geri Keams; illustrated by James Bernardin
Northland, Flagstaff, Arizona. 1995
Grades: All ages

This Cherokee story tells how light was brought to the dark side of the world. Sneaky Coyote convinces the other animals that they should steal a piece of the sun, and shy Possum and cocky Buzzard make attempts with hilarious results. But it is the most unlikely individual—tiny, wise old Grandmother Spider—who has the best idea of all.

Like Jake and Me
by Mavis Jukes; illustrated by Lloyd Bloom
Knopf, New York. 1984
Grades: 2–5

A delightful and heartwarming story about a young boy, Alex, and his stepfather Jake. Alex feels he does not have much in common with Jake and tries desperately to find some way to bridge the gap. In a humorous and surprising way, a hairy wolf spider brings the two of them together. Through the story the reader can learn a great deal about wolf spiders. Also available as a videotape—see the "Resources" section, page 81.

The Magic of Spider Woman
by Lois Duncan; illustrated by Shonto Begay
Scholastic, New York. 1996
Grades: K–4

In this Navajo tale, Wandering Girl, a strong-willed shepherd girl, is taught how to weave blankets by Spider Woman and is given the new name Weaving Woman. Spider Woman warns her never to do too much of anything; to respect boundaries and to keep her life in balance. When Weaving Woman devotes all of her time to a beautiful blanket, something terrible happens. In the end, Weaving Woman learns the value of living a balanced life and teaches her people how to weave.

The Magic School Bus Gets Ants in its Pants: A Book About Ants
TV tie-in book adaptation by Linda Ward Beech and illustrated by
John Speirs; based on *The Magic School Bus* book series written by
Joanna Cole and illustrated by Bruce Degen
Scholastic, New York. 1996
Grades: 1–5

As the class project for the science fair, Ms. Frizzle's class makes a movie
about ants. In the style that has made the Magic School Bus so popular,
the class really "gets into" their project—they shrink and are taken into an
ant hill. The book clearly explains the different jobs ants perform, ant
communication, food sharing, tunnel structure, and life stages. With Ms.
Frizzle's help, the class realizes that the ants work together cooperatively,
and that every ant's job is important for the survival of all. As in other
Magic School Bus books, there is a page of facts in the back of the book,
plus an ant hill project for parents and children.

Night Visitors
by Ed Young
Philomel Books, New York. 1995
Grades: 1–6

When ants invade his family's rice storehouse, young Ho Kuan, who has
great respect for all forms of life, must find a way to seal the storehouse to
keep the ants out before his father kills them all. Through the strong
visions he experiences in a dream—during which he becomes part of an
ant colony—he finds the solution. This book, which is the retelling of a
Chinese folktale, makes a particularly apt connection to the optional
experiments on ant deterrents.

Only Fiona
by Beverly Keller
Harper & Row, New York. 1988
Grades: 4–6

Ten-year-old Fiona Foster is the "new kid" in town and feels alone and
without friends. In the first few chapters, Fiona manages to stop her
parents from spraying ants that have invaded their kitchen. Fiona follows the line of ants to their ant hill and leaves several piles of different
foods there to encourage the ants to stay away from the house. It works,
and Fiona and some new friends gain new respect for ants.

The Spider, the Cave and the Pottery Bowl
by Eleanor Clymer; illustrated by Ingrid Fetz
Atheneum, New York. 1972
Grades: 3–6

Kate and Johnny are sent to the mesa to spend the summer with their
ailing grandmother. One evening grandmother tells stories—one about
how the people came to the mesa, one about why ants have thin waists,
and one about Grandmother Spider. The next day, on the far side of the
mesa, the children discover Grandmother Spider's secret house behind
which is a hidden supply of fine clay in a small cave. They take some
clay to their grandmother who then teaches them how to make pots as
beautiful as those made by their ancestors. When Kate discovers Grandmother Spider's home by a spring, she thinks "How clever she was to
make her web by the spring where the flies would come" demonstrating
the relation of an animal's chosen habitat to environmental factors.

Two Bad Ants
by Chris Van Allsburg
Houghton Mifflin Co., Boston. 1988
Grades: Preschool–4

A colony of ants follows in a line behind a scout ant who leads them to
get beautiful sparkling crystals (sugar) for their queen. When the colony
departs, two curious ants stay behind. After surviving many life-threat-
ening situations, the two ants become convinced they should return to the
safety of their colony. Students could answer the question, "How was the
scout able to find her way back to the sugar in order to lead the colony to
it?"

Why Spiders Spin: A Story of Arachne
retold by Jamie and Scott Simons; illustrated by Deborah Winograd
Silver Press, Engelwood Cliffs, New Jersey. 1991
Grades: 2—5

This is a retelling of the Greek myth about Arachne, a weaver of fine and
beautiful cloth. By boasting about the quality of her weaving, she angers
the goddess Athena who challenges her to a contest. Seeing that
Arachne's weaving is indeed on a level with her own and angered by the
images portrayed in Arachne's weaving, Athena turns the young lady
into a spider—destined to spin forever and weave a lonely web.

Summary Outlines

Activity 1: Exploring the Schoolyard Study Area

Getting Ready

Before the Day of the Activity
1. Choose an area with diverse vegetation and physical features.
2. Take a tour of the area to be aware of any potential hazards.
3. Plan to hold class discussions inside whenever possible.
4. Make a map of the study area on an overhead transparency. Include compass and scale. Draw and label highly visible features.
5. Make a copy of the map for each student.
6. Make an enlarged version of the map.
7. Make a clipboard for each student.
8. Obtain or have students make journals.

On the Day of the Activity
1. Post the large map of study area.
2. Have student maps and clipboards ready for distribution.

Introducing the Activity
1. Students are scientists studying animals and plants that live in schoolyard.
2. Introduce large map.
3. Ask what living things (besides people) students have seen in study area.
4. They will first learn more about study area itself, not the animals. A place where things may live is called an **environment.**
5. Encourage students to observe, using sight, smell, hearing, and touch.
6. Ask students to name warmest and coolest parts of schoolyard.
7. Ask what else might be important to living things. List as "Environmental Factors." Scientists try to find out how these factors affect living things.
8. Be sure the list includes sunlight, moisture (or wetness), and cover.

Explaining the Challenge
1. Tell students they will use their senses to observe all environmental factors listed, especially three factors—**sunlight, moisture, and cover.**
2. Explain that students will work in pairs focusing on only **one** factor.
3. Assign one third of the pairs to each environmental factor.
4. If they're studying sunlight, they should find three sunniest places and three shadiest places in study area, and mark them on maps by writing "sunny" or "shady."
5. Model how to record on maps.
6. Check to be sure the "moisture" and "cover" teams know what to record.
7. Distribute clipboards and a map to each student.

Exploring Sunlight, Moisture, Cover

1. Gather class on yard. Ask everyone to locate where they are standing on their map.
2. Have everyone find north on map, then turn to face north on schoolyard. Where are south, east, and west?
3. Point to a prominent feature and ask them to locate it on their maps.
4. Ask a volunteer to review how they'll map environmental factors.
5. Emphasize they'll be "on the job" as scientists—they should walk quietly and carefully observe the environment.
6. Circulate, giving assistance as needed. Encourage teams who finish early to observe other factors from class list.
7. Return to classroom.

Back in the Classroom

1. Have students share interesting discoveries about temperature, air movement, sounds, other factors.
2. Praise their efforts. Scientists often begin studying an area by mapping environmental factors.
3. Some student discoveries about sunlight, moisture, and cover will be recorded on large map. Each pair of students reports two spots they recorded on their maps.
4. As pairs discuss which two spots to report, make a key near one edge of your large map. Write "Moisture," "Sunlight," and "Cover" with different color markers, with blue for "Moisture."
5. Point out the key. Explain that you will use a blue "plus" sign to mark a wet spot, and a blue "minus" sign for dry. Ask pairs that studied moisture to share their data, and record.
6. If students seem unsure about the placement of their data, prompt them with landmarks and directions.
7. Following color key, use plus and minus signs to record student data on sun/shade and cover/open. When all have reported, ask, "What can we say about the environmental factor of moisture (sunlight, cover) based on the class data?"
8. Ask, "How do you think time of day might affect some of the marks?" "What about time of year?"
9. Ask, "If we go back out to the study area tomorrow, where do you think we'll find the most insects?" "The least?" "Why?" Accept all responses.
10. Explain that **ecologists** are scientists who study the environment *and* the living things in it. Students are schoolyard ecologists.

Journal Writing

1. Distribute journals.
2. Remind students to write the date and time on top of journal page.
3. Have students write things that interested them and questions they have.

Activity 2: Finding and Observing Spiders

Getting Ready
1. Duplicate a page of Animal ID Cards or each student, plus a few extra.
2. Read about spiders in "Behind the Scenes."
3. Decide whether you'll do the Spider Web Identification activity. If so, copy the Spider Web Identification Key and provide additional time in study area.

Introducing the Activity
1. Students will locate and observe spiders.
2. Share a story, pictures, or some fun spider facts.
3. Invite discussion of positive things about spiders, and ways to lessen fear.
4. Ask students where they've seen spiders in study area.
5. Point out that spiders are often secretive.
6. Ask students to help you list clues to their presence.
7. Each student should fill out an ID card for each spider, drawing and writing what they actually see.
8. Be sure students know not to touch spiders.
9. Walk to study area, taking a spray bottle of water.

Observing Spiders
1. Circulate, encouraging discoveries. Use spray bottle to mist webs.
2. Encourage students to look for webs, egg cases, and evidence of insect meals. Have them observe and report on spider behavior.
3. Remind students to draw and describe spiders and webs on their ID cards.
4. Remind them to mark locations of spider activity on their maps.
5. After about 15–20 minutes, return to classroom.

Recording Spider Locations on the Class Map
1. Discuss students' discoveries.
2. Consider briefly introducing information on spiders.
3. Draw a spider symbol in new color marker (or apply a stick-on dot) on key of class map and write "Spider" next to it.
4. Each pair draws spider symbol (or uses dot) to record a place they found a spider or evidence of spider activity. Pairs take turns while rest of class is writing.
5. Give class 10–15 minutes to complete Animal ID Cards and write in journals.
6. After all have recorded, discuss ideas about spider distribution.
7. Ask students to look at data for moisture, sunlight, and cover. "Where are the greatest numbers of spiders?" "Why might that be?" "What environmental factors seem to influence the spiders?"
8. Congratulate students for thinking like ecologists about how living things and the environment may be connected.

Activity 3: Discovering Animal Communities

Getting Ready
1. Make one shake box for each pair of students.
2. Practice using a shake box outdoors before the activity.
3. Duplicate a page of Animal ID Cards for each student, plus a few extra.

Introducing the Activity in the Classroom
1. Ask what kinds of animals they've seen in the schoolyard, and list.
2. Today they will again be ecologists, looking for small animals.
3. Focus on class map. Ask where they think they'll find the most small animals. They should consider environmental factors. Accept all predictions.
4. Ask where they found the most spiders. "What do you think spiders eat?" Suggest that other small animals may be found nearby.
5. Tell students they can carefully turn over rocks and leaves to find animals.
6. Say you will show them how to use a shake box outside.
7. Point on the large map to the location of your shake box demonstration.
8. Distribute Animal ID Cards and other materials and walk to the study site.

Modeling the Shake Box Outside
1. Gather the class around vegetation in the study area.
2. Model how to use a shake box.
3. Stress the importance of recording observations.
4. If they find tiny animals that are hard to see, you'll lend them a magnifying lens.
5. They'll have about 20–30 minutes to collect, observe, record, and release animals.

Sampling with Shake Boxes in the Study Area
1. Distribute shake boxes and have students begin.
2. Circulate, noting discoveries and encouraging them to share collecting and recording.
3. Encourage pairs to show each other what they found.
4. Be sure students release their animals where they were collected.

Back in the Classroom
1. Give students a few minutes to finish Animal ID Cards.
2. Hold a class discussion of their findings.
3. Make additions to the class list of animals.
4. Introduce the concept of **animal communities**—a variety of different animals that live in the same area and depend on each other for food and other things.
5. Ask students to name several different animals found on one plant. These make up a small **community.** Some animals depend on the plant

for food; the plant also provides shelter for other animals that feed on the plant-eating animals.

6. Have students give other examples of small schoolyard communities.

Recording Locations of Animals on the Class Map

1. Add "Animals" to the key of your large class map, using a different color marker and a symbol to represent all animals found (except spiders).

2. While class is writing, pairs of students take turns recording one place they found an animal.

3. Give students 10–15 minutes to write and draw in their journals.

4. Once all pairs have recorded data on map, ask questions to elicit comments or conclusions about locations of animals and spiders and their relation to each other.

Sorting the Animal ID Cards

1. Students sort ID cards in different ways. Each time they do a sort, they must agree as a group on characteristic used.

2. Give example: "If I wanted to sort all of you into two different groups, I might have everyone wearing red move to that corner, and those people not wearing red move to this corner."

3. Ask for examples of ways to group animals. Distribute scissors and have students cut apart and pool Animal ID Cards.

4. Have students sort.

5. When all finish at least one sort, ask some to describe a way they sorted.

6. Explain that ecologists work in the same way they just did.

7. With older students, consider a dichotomous sort.

Activity 4: Tracking Ants

Getting Ready

1. Cut sponge into small pieces, one for each group. Put pieces in ziplock bag to soak with juice or non-diet soda.

2. Use spoon or popsicle stick to put small amounts of jelly, graham cracker, and cat food on a lid for each group. Add soaked sponge piece to each lid. Put lids and toothpicks on a tray.

3. Check study area to make sure there are ant trails. If ants are scarce, put small dabs of cat food or jelly in various spots a day ahead of time.

4. Copy Ant Challenges student sheet for each student.

Introducing the Ant Activity

1. Focus on large map. Ask students where they have seen ants. What were the ants doing?

2. Encourage them to share general experiences with ants.

3. Point out that ants often come in conflict with people. Ants are good at surviving in our environments and can be found almost everywhere on land.
4. Explain that their goal as ecologists is to find out more about ant behavior.

Explaining the Activity

1. Lines of ants are called "ant trails." They will find an ant trail to study, first marking its location on their maps.
2. Distribute student sheet, and read the four challenges. After conducting and recording the first three, they will get food samples from you for the fourth challenge.
3. When they get the food, groups should make predictions and decide together which foods to use.
4. Caution students not to dump globs of food on top of ants.
5. Explain that sponge has been soaked in soda (or juice) and they will squeeze small amounts of juice alongside ant trail or place sponge beside trail.
6. Walk to study area with needed materials.

Tracking Ants on the Schoolyard

1. Circulate, noting observations and reminding all students to record. Ask questions to help focus detailed observations.
2. When groups have conducted and recorded first three challenges, have them take toothpicks and a lid of food samples. They should discuss their ideas and plan before putting food everywhere.
3. Lend assistance if needed.
4. Encourage students to visit other experiments.
5. Give students five minute warning to finish and record experiments.

Back in the Classroom

1. Have groups choose a reporter and decide what ant behavior they would like to report.
2. Let groups share findings. What new questions did ant studies bring up?
3. Have students write in journals.

Activity 5: Special Study Sites

Getting Ready

1. For each string loop, cut three-yard length and tie ends. Wind each loop around cardboard or stick so it won't get tangled. Leave one unwound for demonstration.
2. If using, duplicate ID cards for each student, plus a few extra.

Introducing the Activity

1. Students will apply ecological skills to a smaller study site.
2. Hold up a string loop that will enclose site. They can adjust shape of string to include as many interesting things as possible.
3. Model procedure on a table in the classroom.
4. Once they choose loop location, they'll mark it on maps.
5. On chalkboard, draw a shape like your string loop. Inside it, draw and label a spider, a leaf, a few pebbles. They'll draw their personal site on a piece of unlined paper.
6. After observing site, they'll write about it.
7. They'll focus on their site for about 20 minutes.
8. Go to study area and have students select their site.

On the Schoolyard

1. As students choose spots, remind them to mark location on map, then observe and record carefully.
2. Circulate, offering Animal ID Cards and magnifiers.
3. When finished, have students rewind loops and return to classroom.

Back in the Classroom

1. Ask students to share discoveries.
2. Have students reflect on why they found (or didn't find) animals in their site, given environmental conditions. Encourage them to suggest what factors might be influencing plants and animals.
3. Ask students if they chose sites with lots of cover. How many found animals there? What about open sites? Which had the most animals?
4. Ask students how their personal site might change over time and write about it in their journals.
5. Consider the "Going Further" suggestions.

Animal ID   Date _____

Name _____

Kind of Animal _____

Describe it:

Draw it:

Number of animals _____

Animal ID   Date _____

Name _____

Kind of Animal _____

Describe it:

Draw it:

Number of animals _____

Animal ID   Date _____

Name _____

Kind of Animal _____

Describe it:

Draw it:

Number of animals _____

Animal ID   Date _____

Name _____

Kind of Animal _____

Describe it:

Draw it:

Number of animals _____

Ant Challenges

1. **Observe:** Watch an ant trail. (Don't disturb the ants.) What do you see?

2. **Road Block:** Gently put something across the ant trail. What do the ants do?

3. **Take Away:** Carefully use a leaf or stick to move one ant a few feet away from the ant trail. What does the ant do?

4. **Food Tests:** Put a small amount of food near the ant trail. Watch for a while. What happens?